For all the flaws I've colored

scan to see more

To see more Fat Art Follow me
instagram: @Colormyflaws
www.patreon.com/ffwb

For permission and to learn more contact colormyflaws@gmail.com

Select Prints available upon request

Author : Isaac Snagg
ISBN : 9798780851325

All rights reserved.
No part of this book may be reproduced or used
in any manner without the prior written permission
of the copyright owner, except for the use of brief quotations
for review.

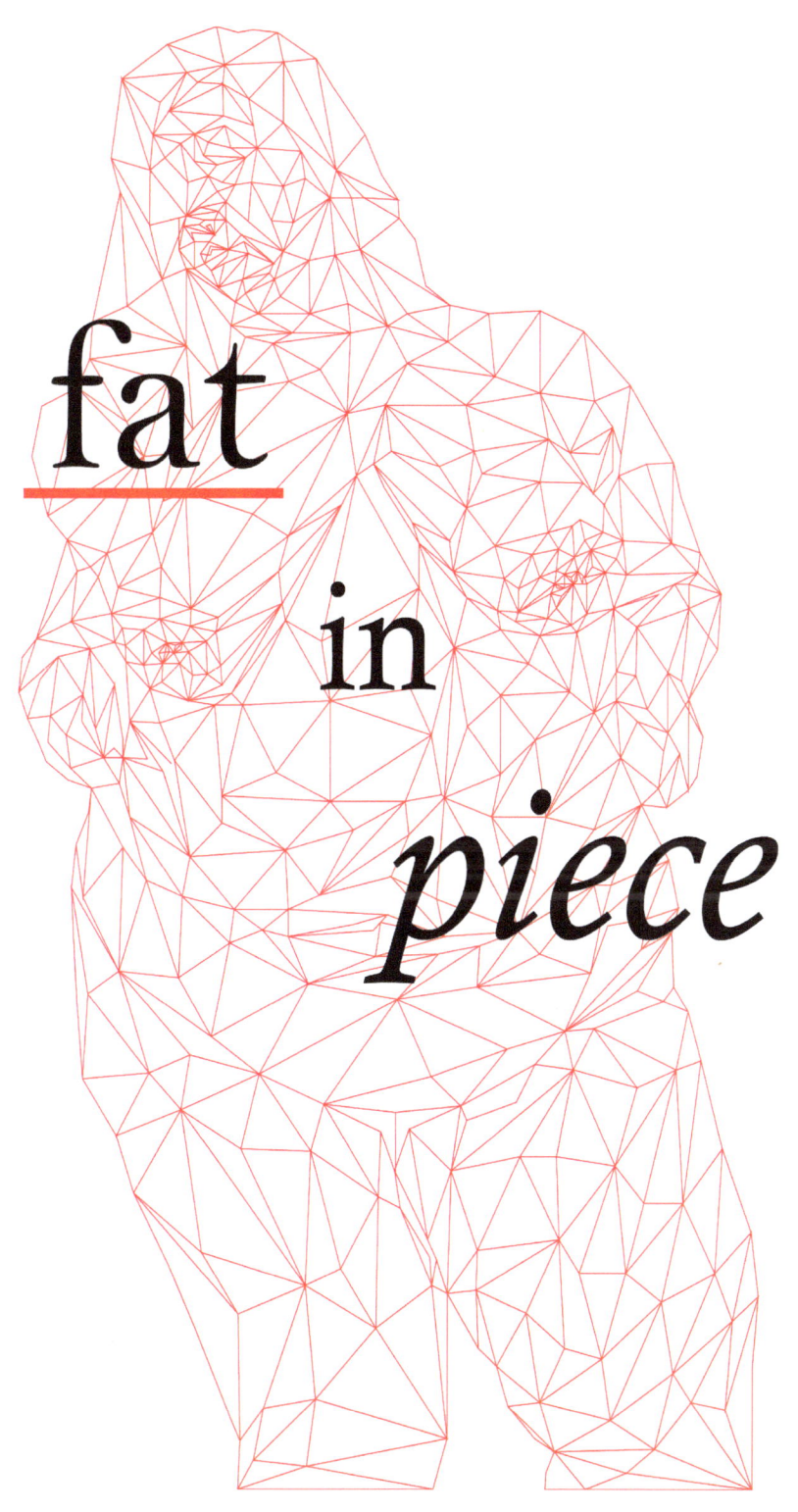

Fat bodies deserve a space to be seen as beautiful in peace. There is so much heavy baggage in society when it comes to how we handle fat bodies. From extreme distaste to obsence fetishism, it's difficult to be seen as just a human being. In this book I want you to see humans existing as fat and beautiful beings, seen through my eyes as an artist.

Each one of us is molded by the experiences we face every day. Each heart break and victory come together to shape who we are and how we perceive this world we share. I choose this fractal style in my illustrations because it breaks down complex images into simple polygonal shapes, which alone mean nothing to the eye, but together build a decipherable image. Likewise, you and I are a collection of pieces that when viewed alone don't tell a full story, but when viewed as a whole reveals something beautiful.

Words By Isaac Snagg

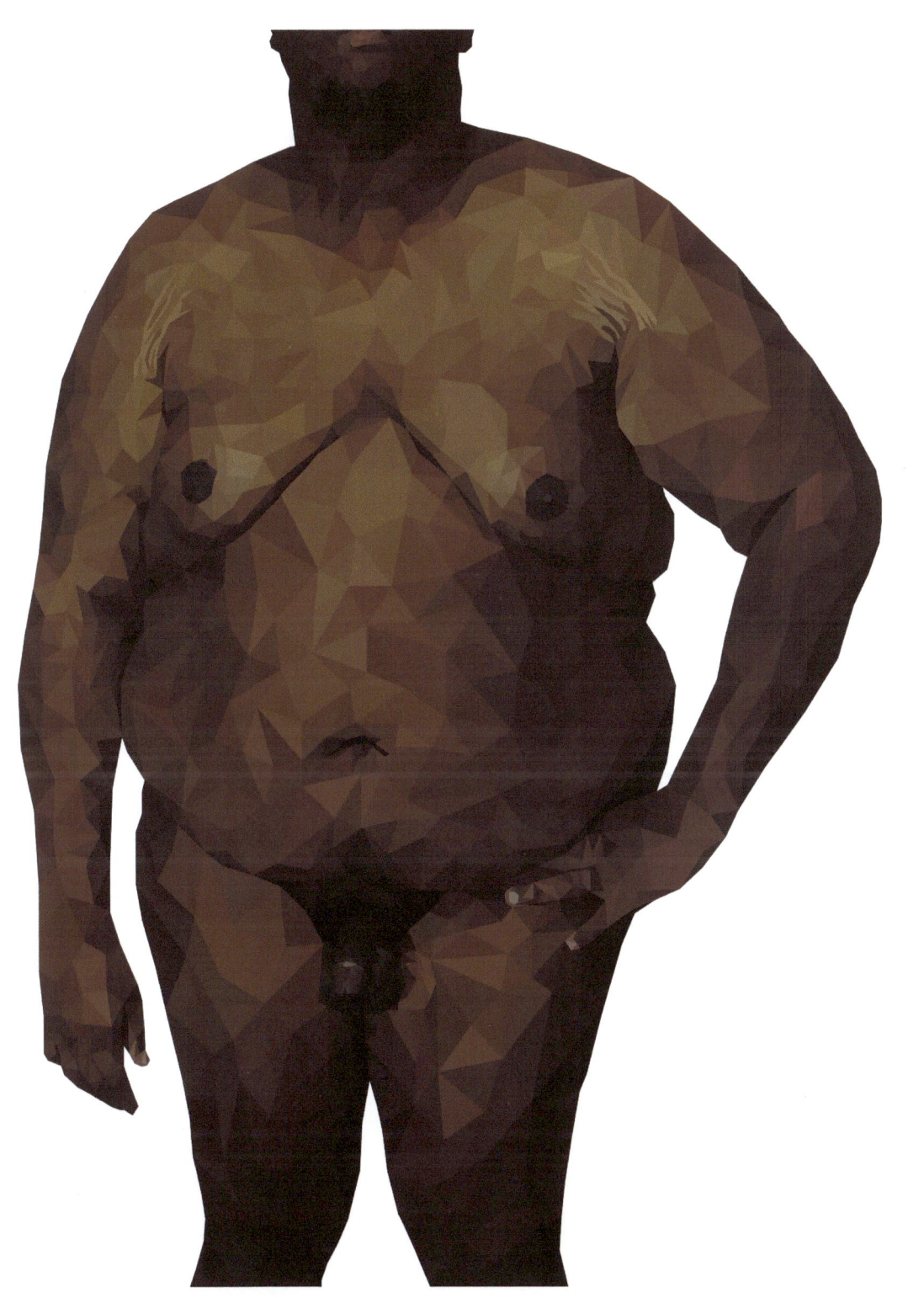

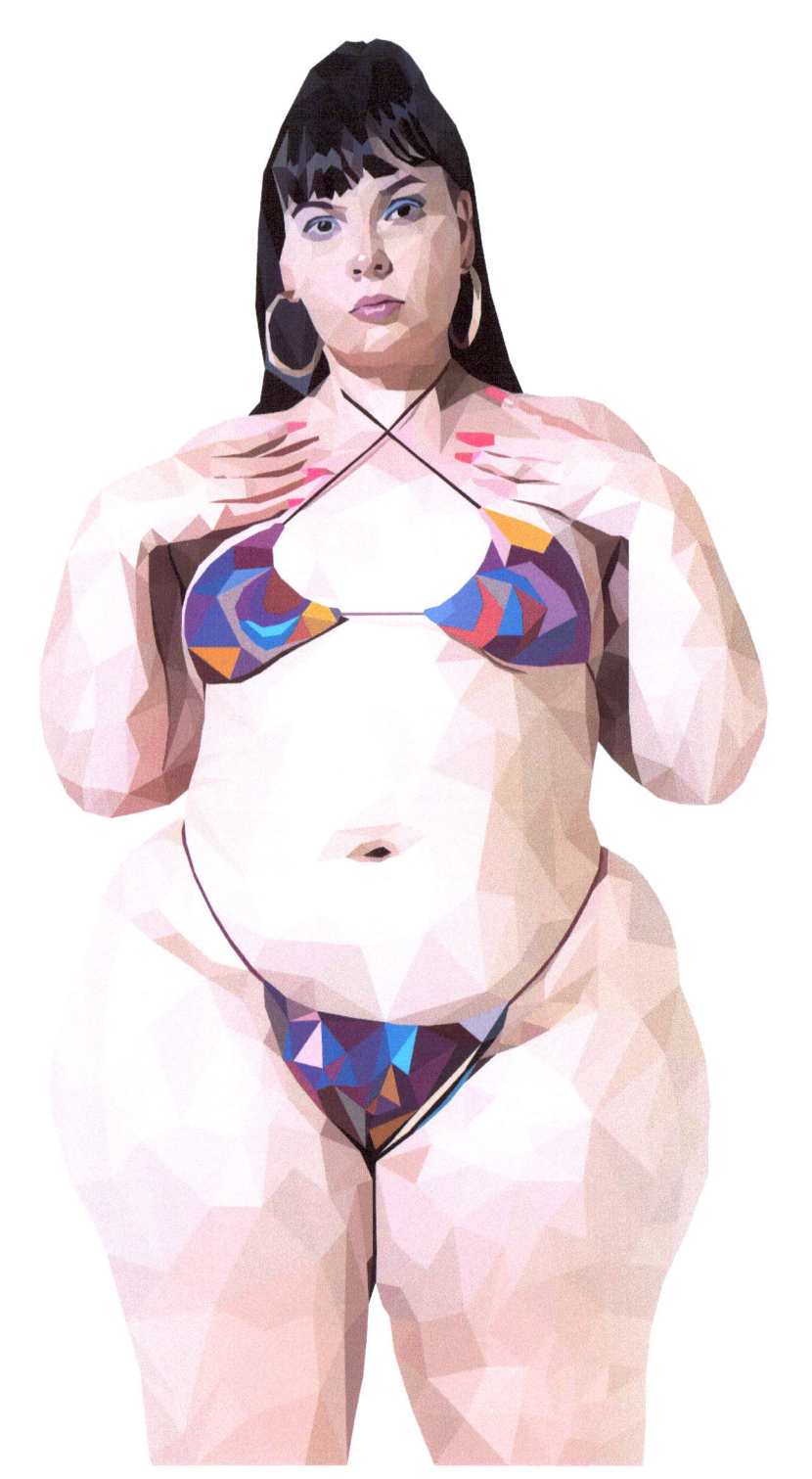

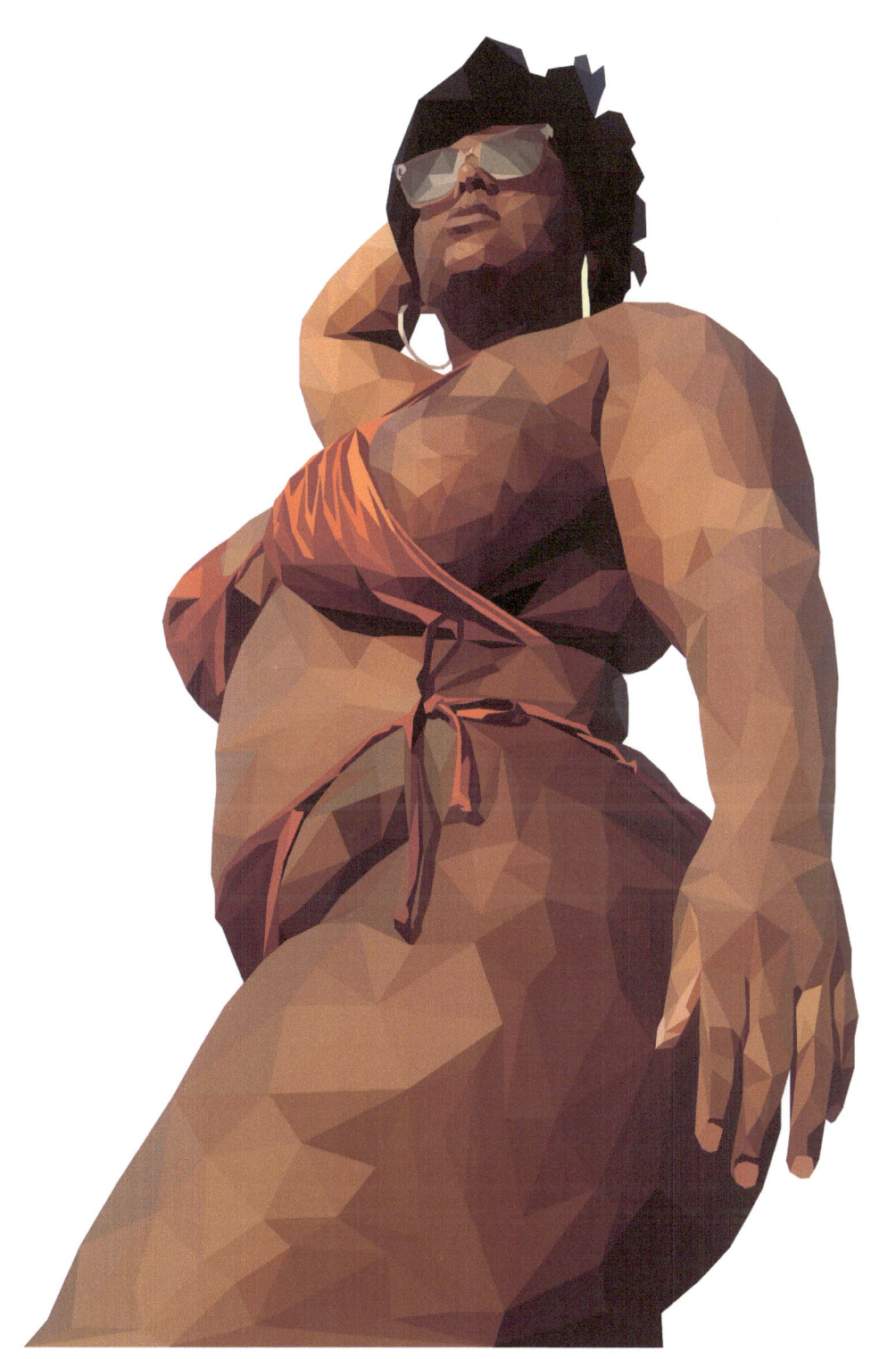

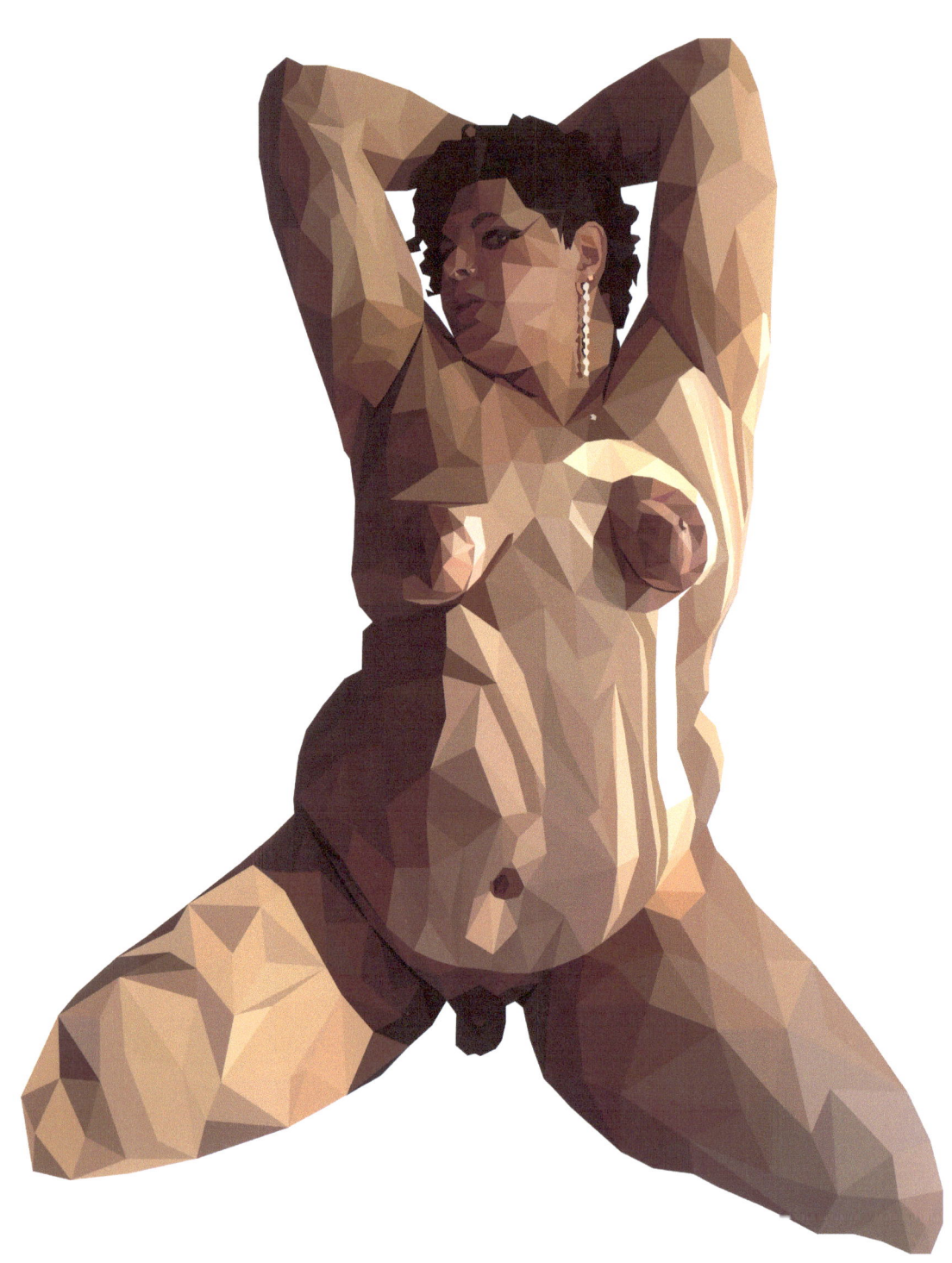

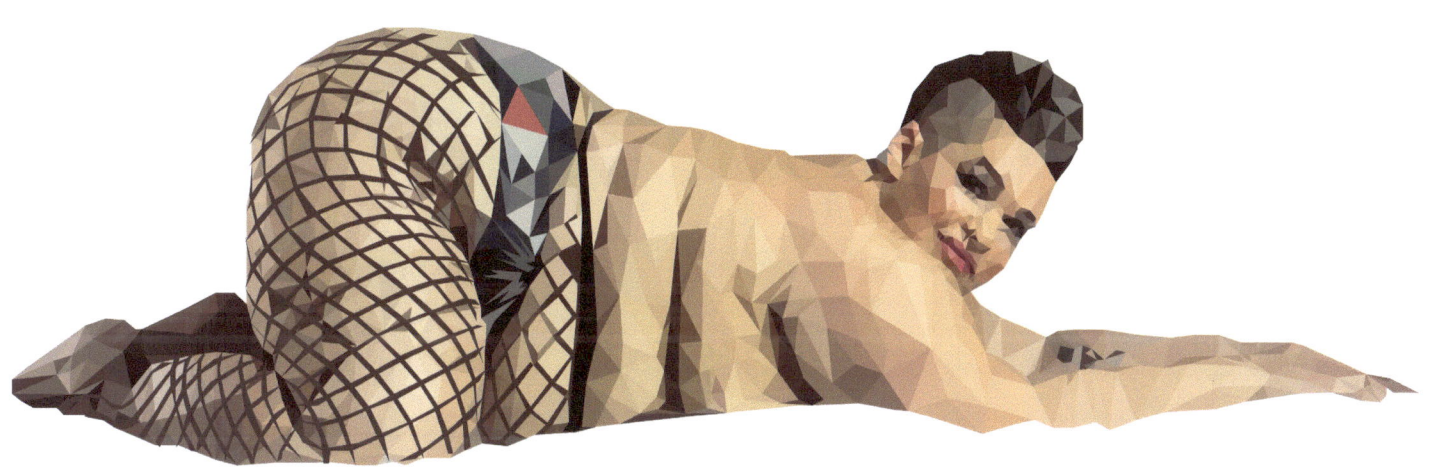

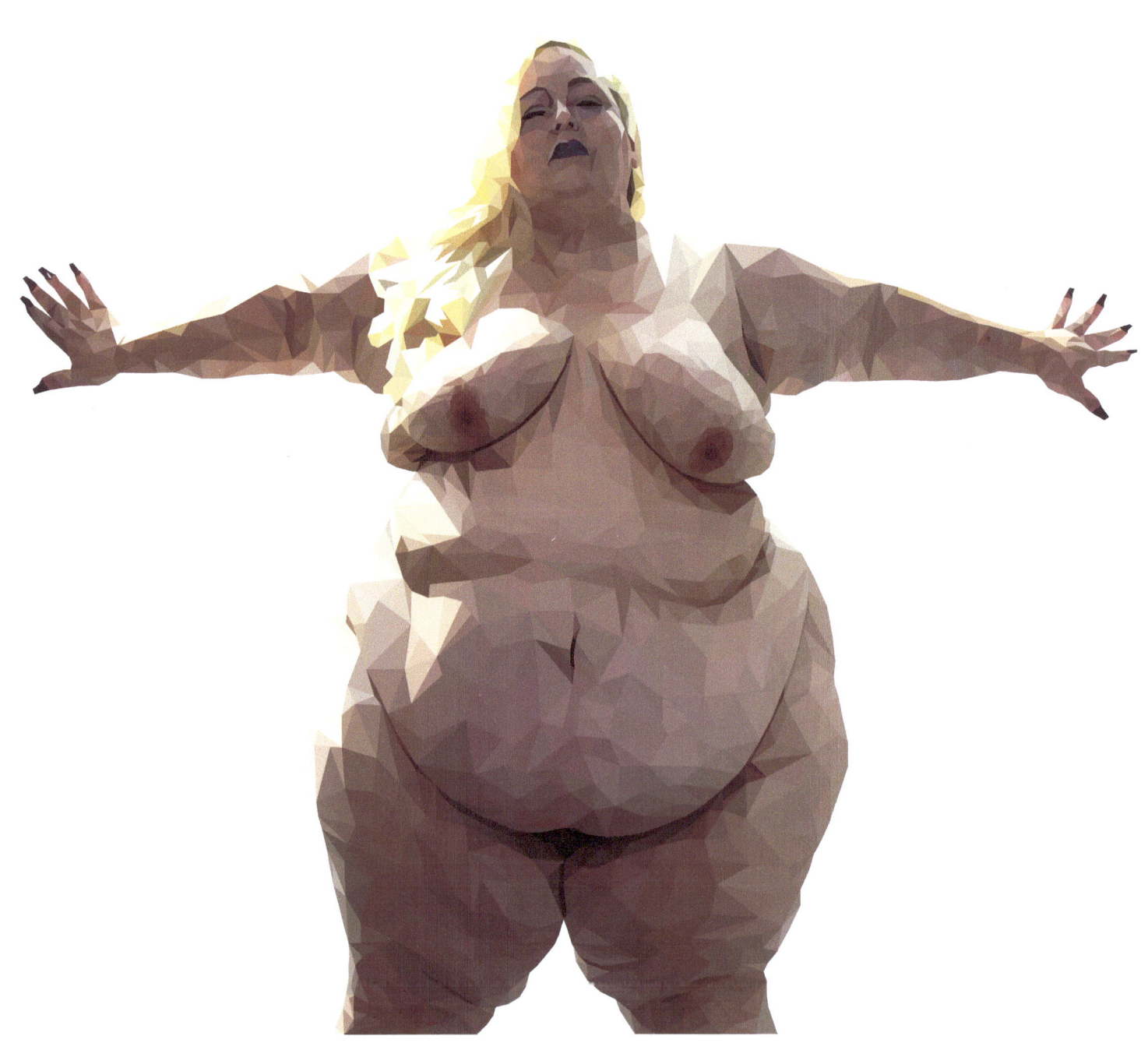

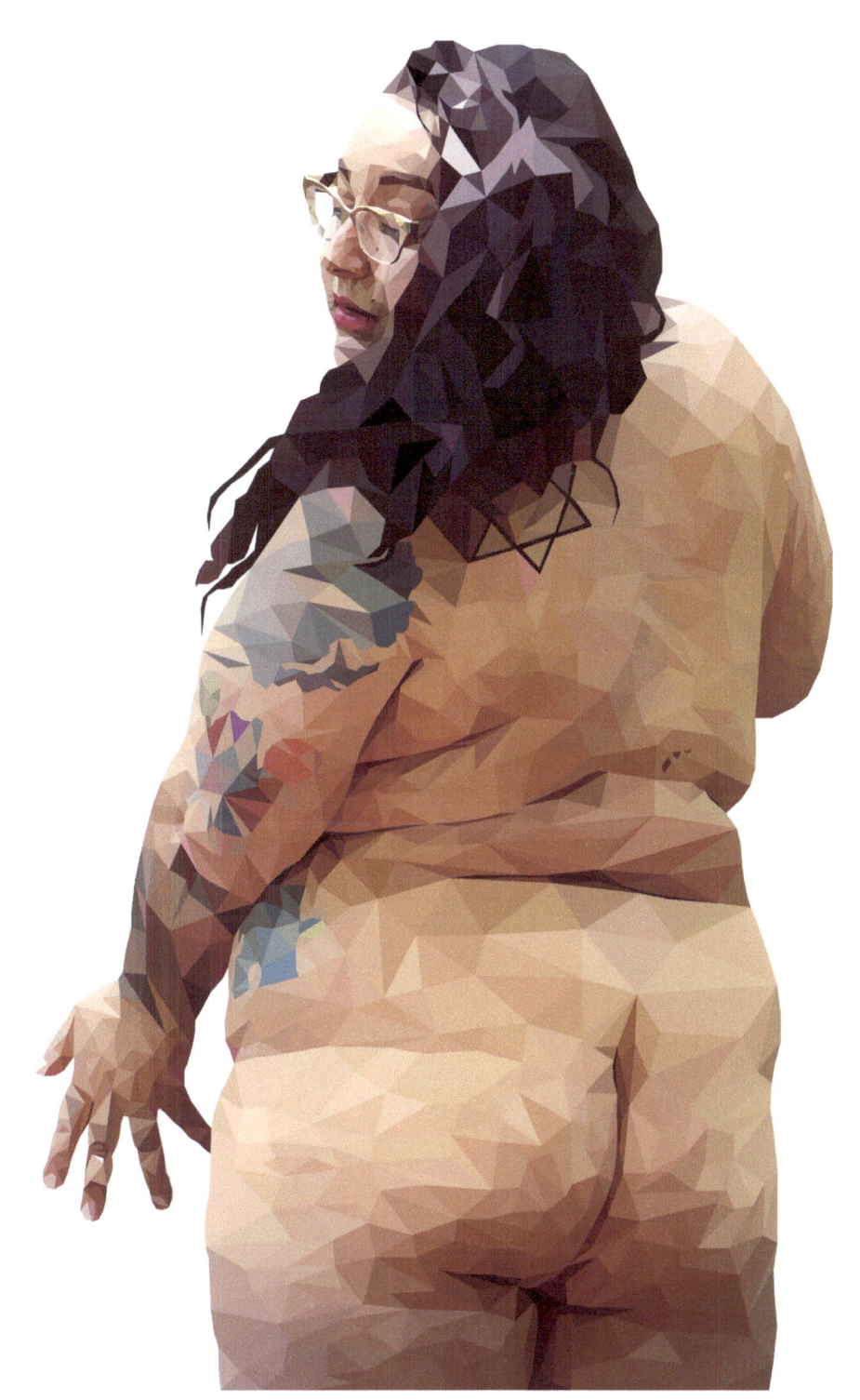

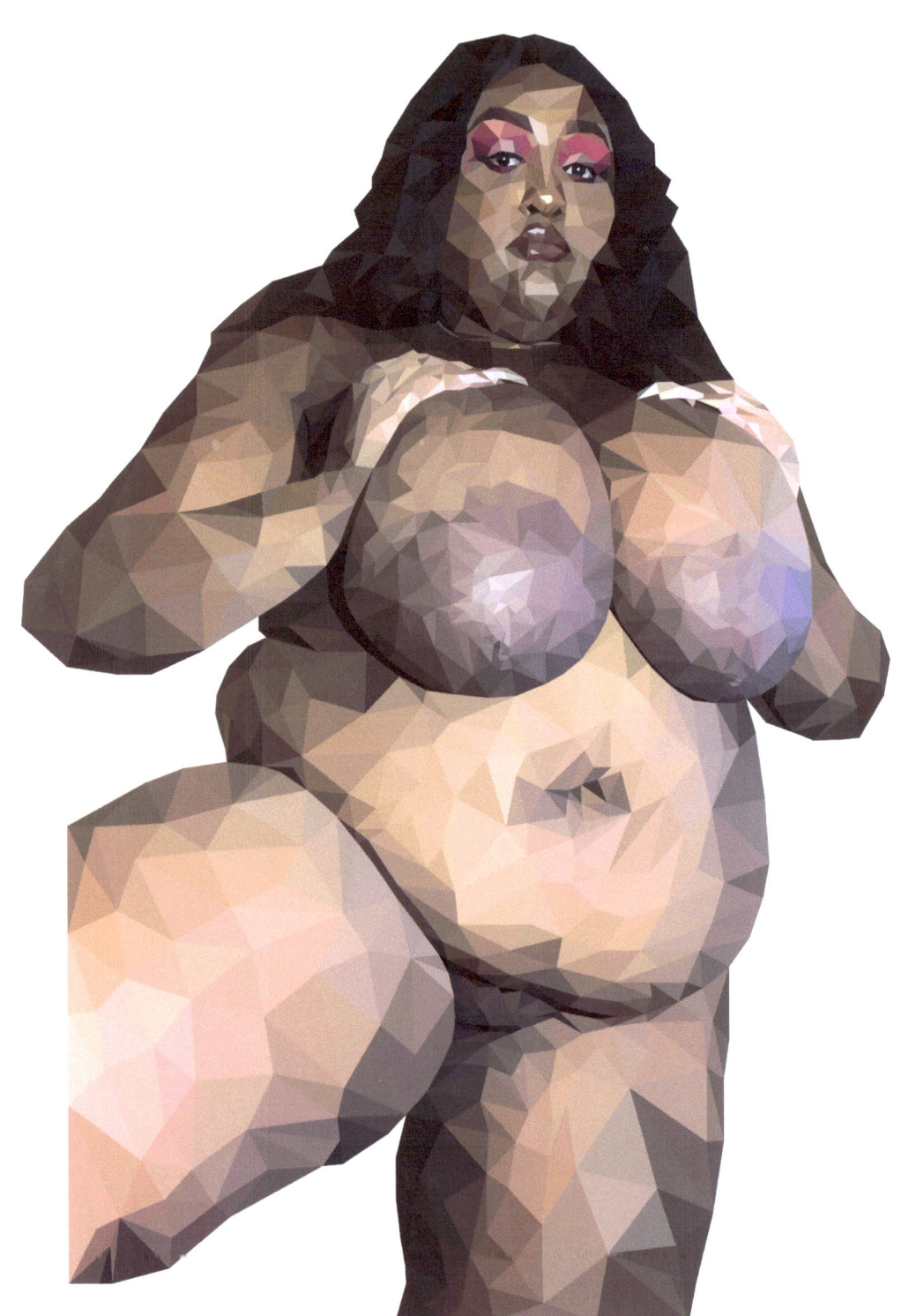

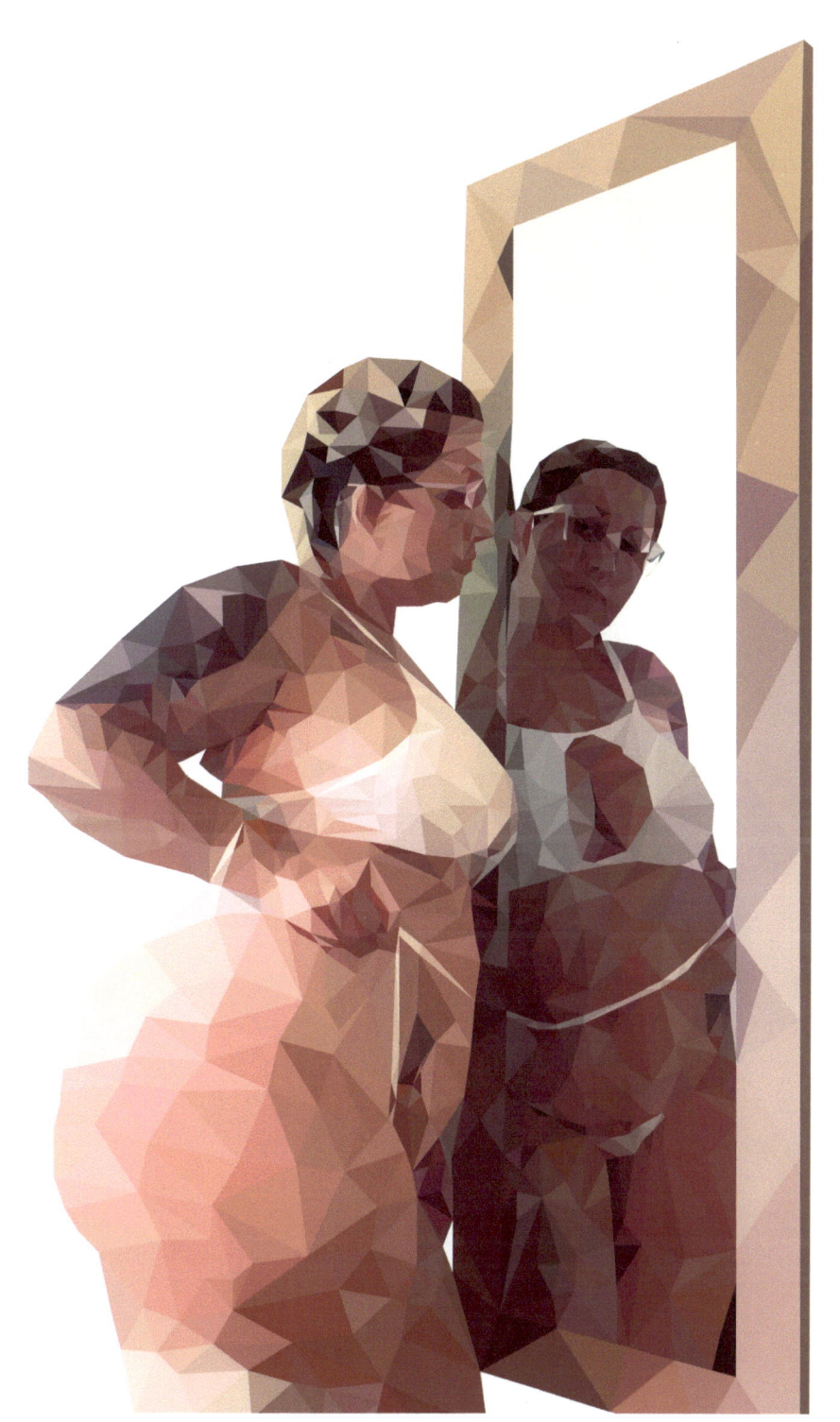

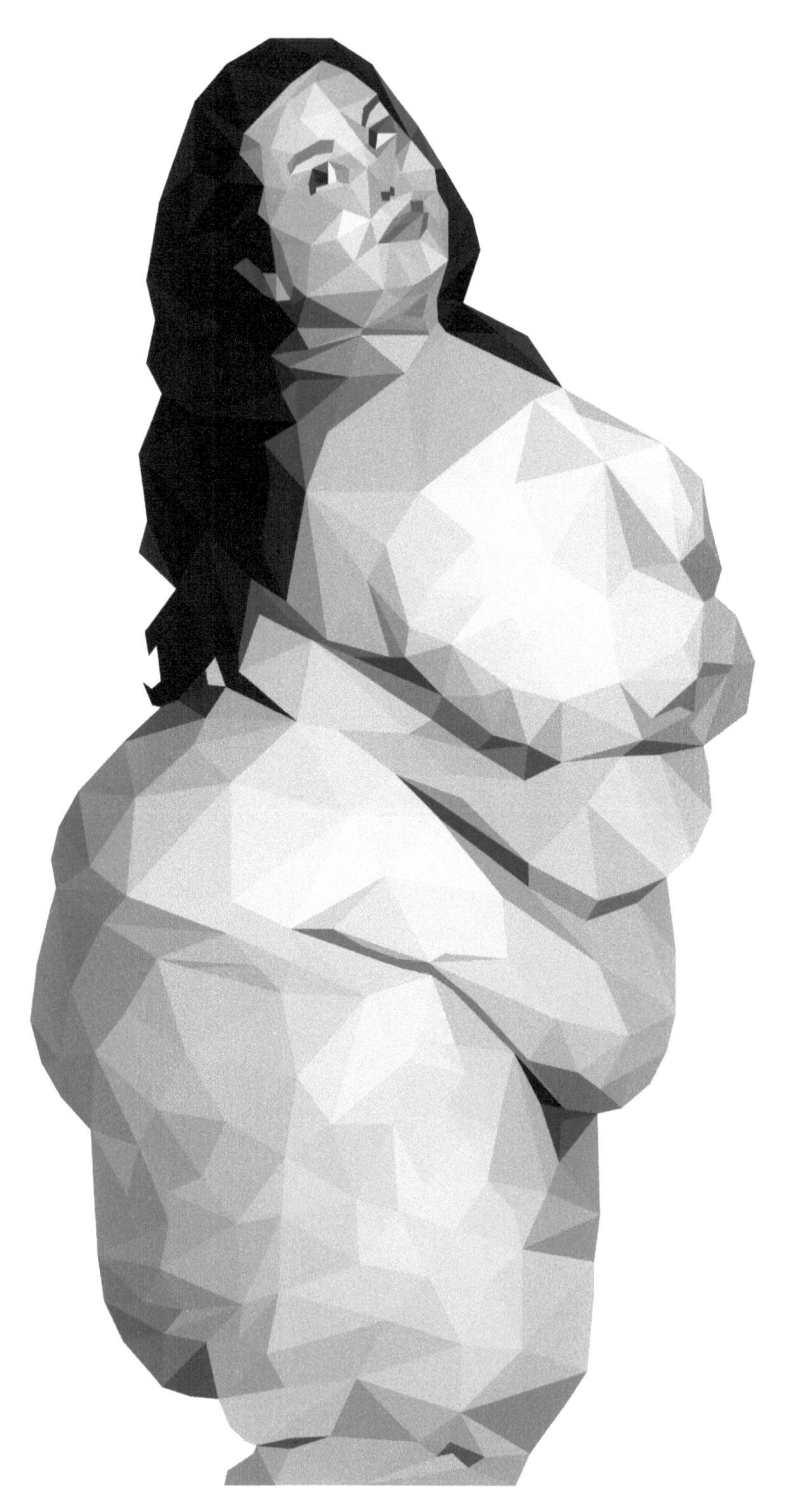

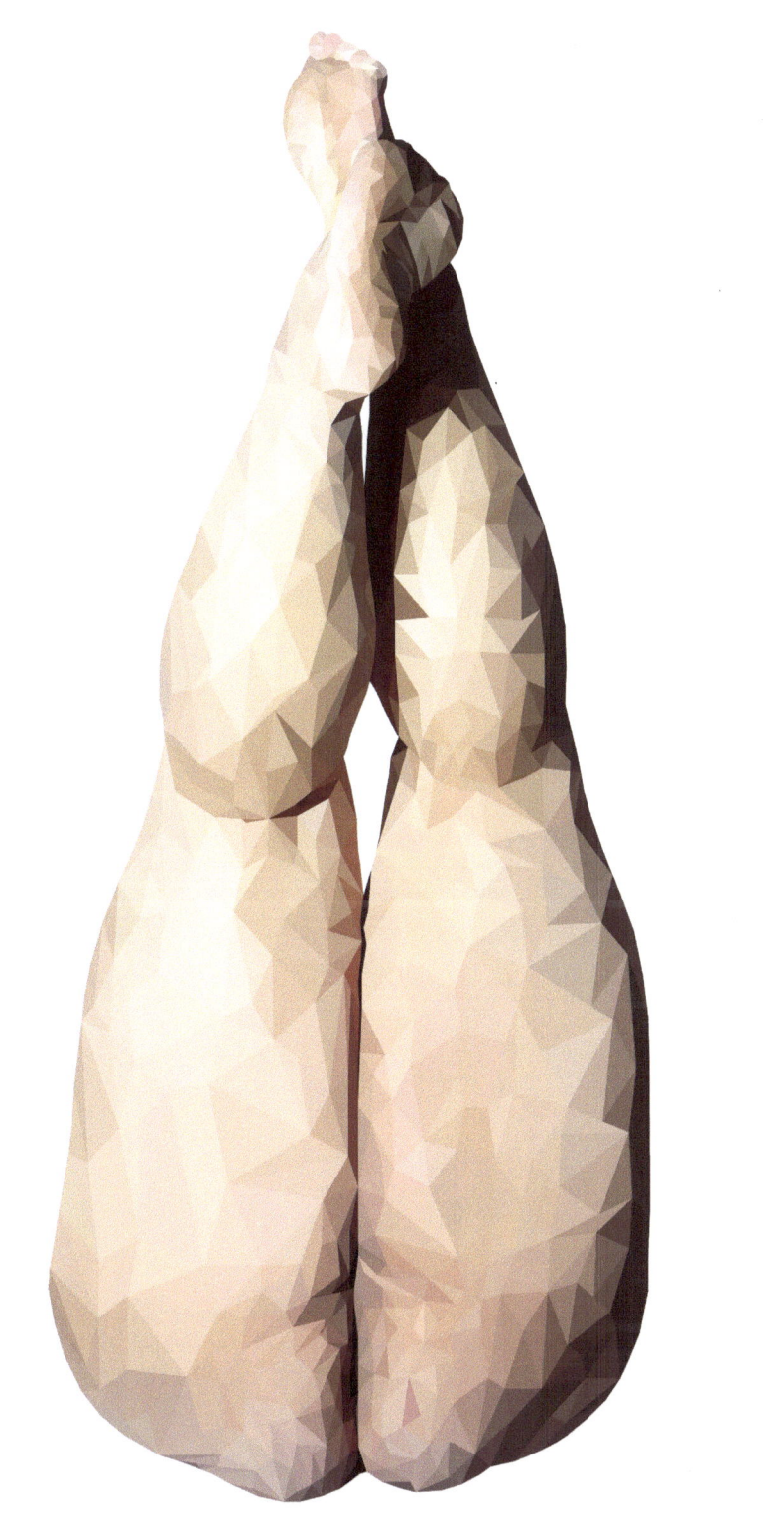

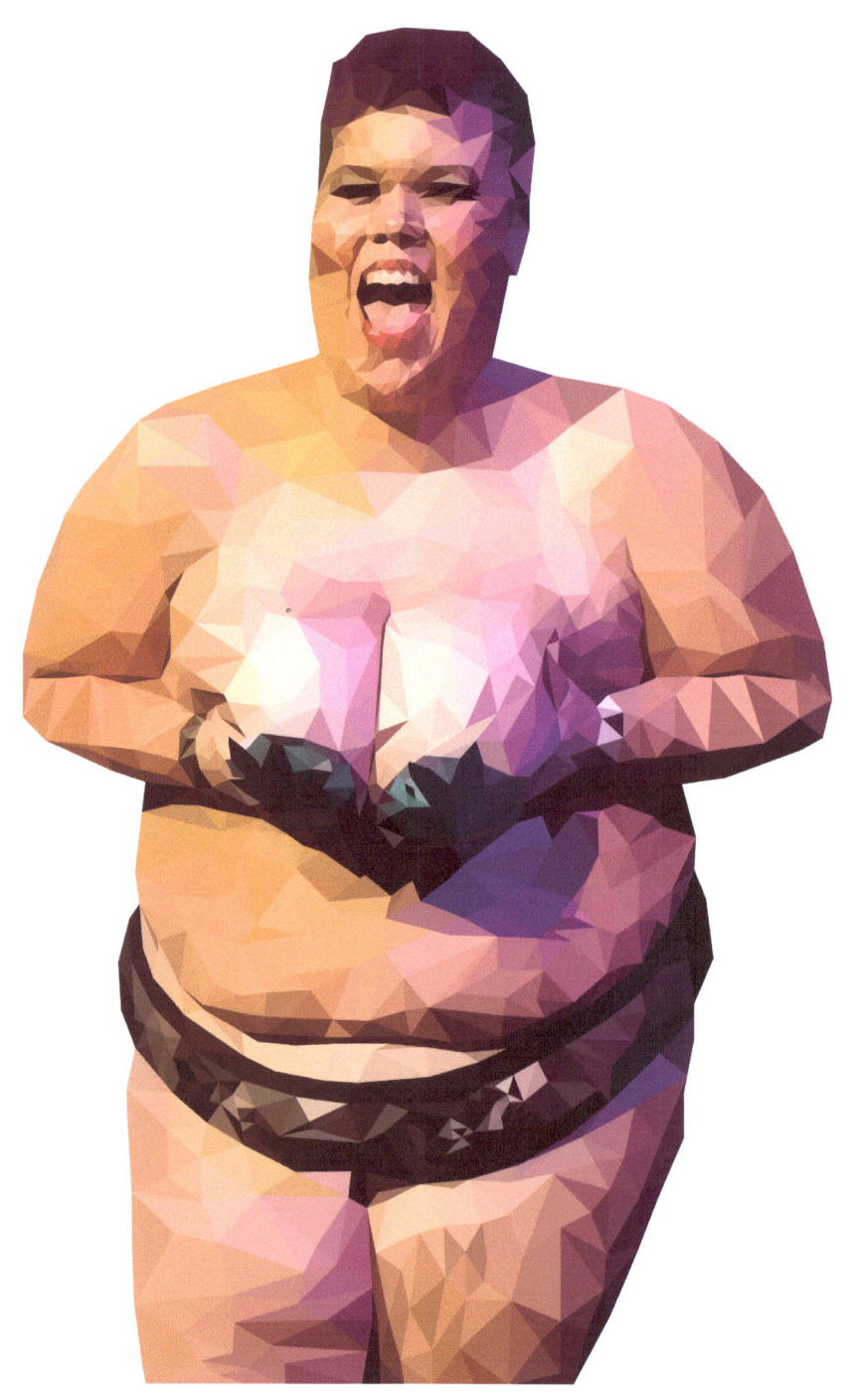

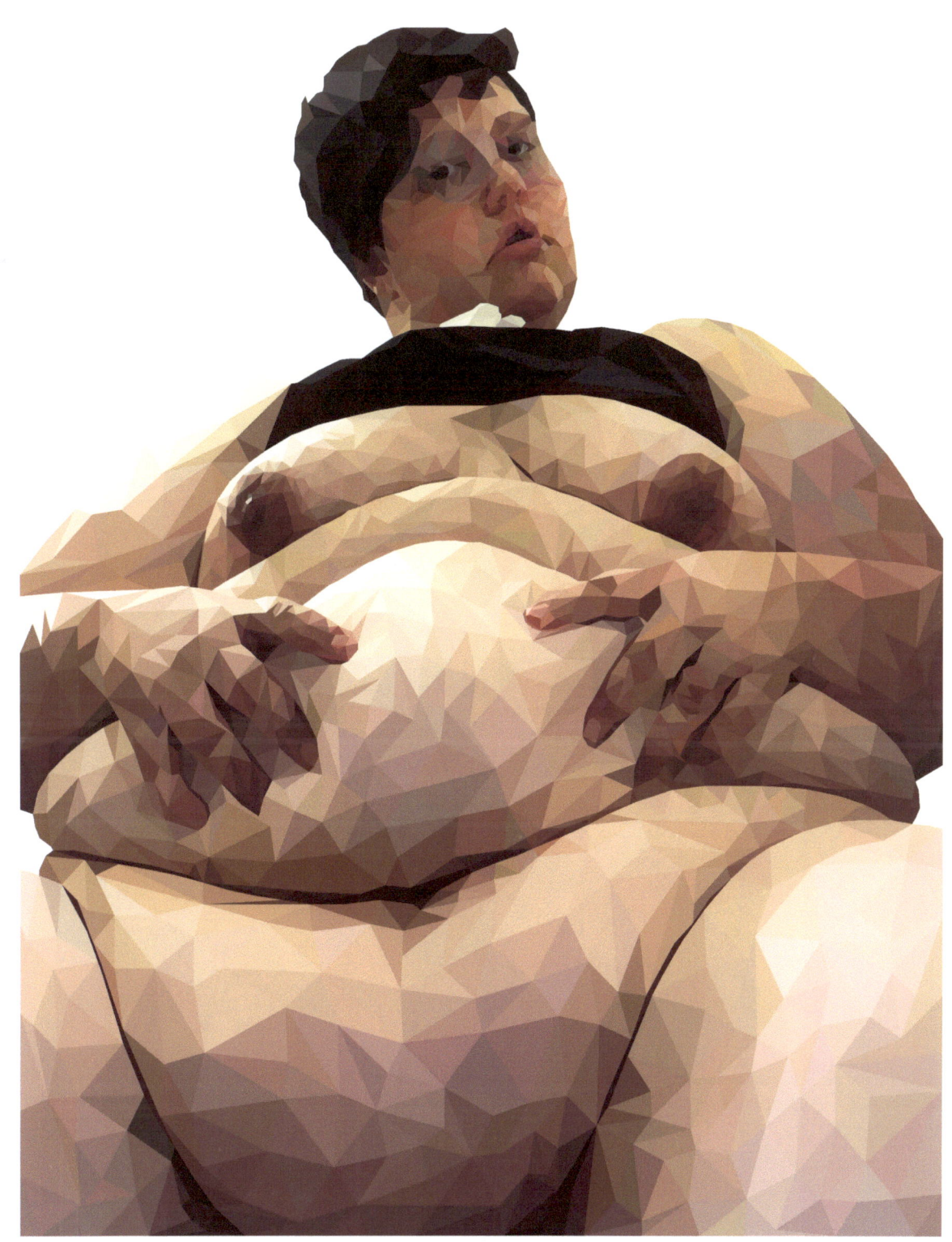

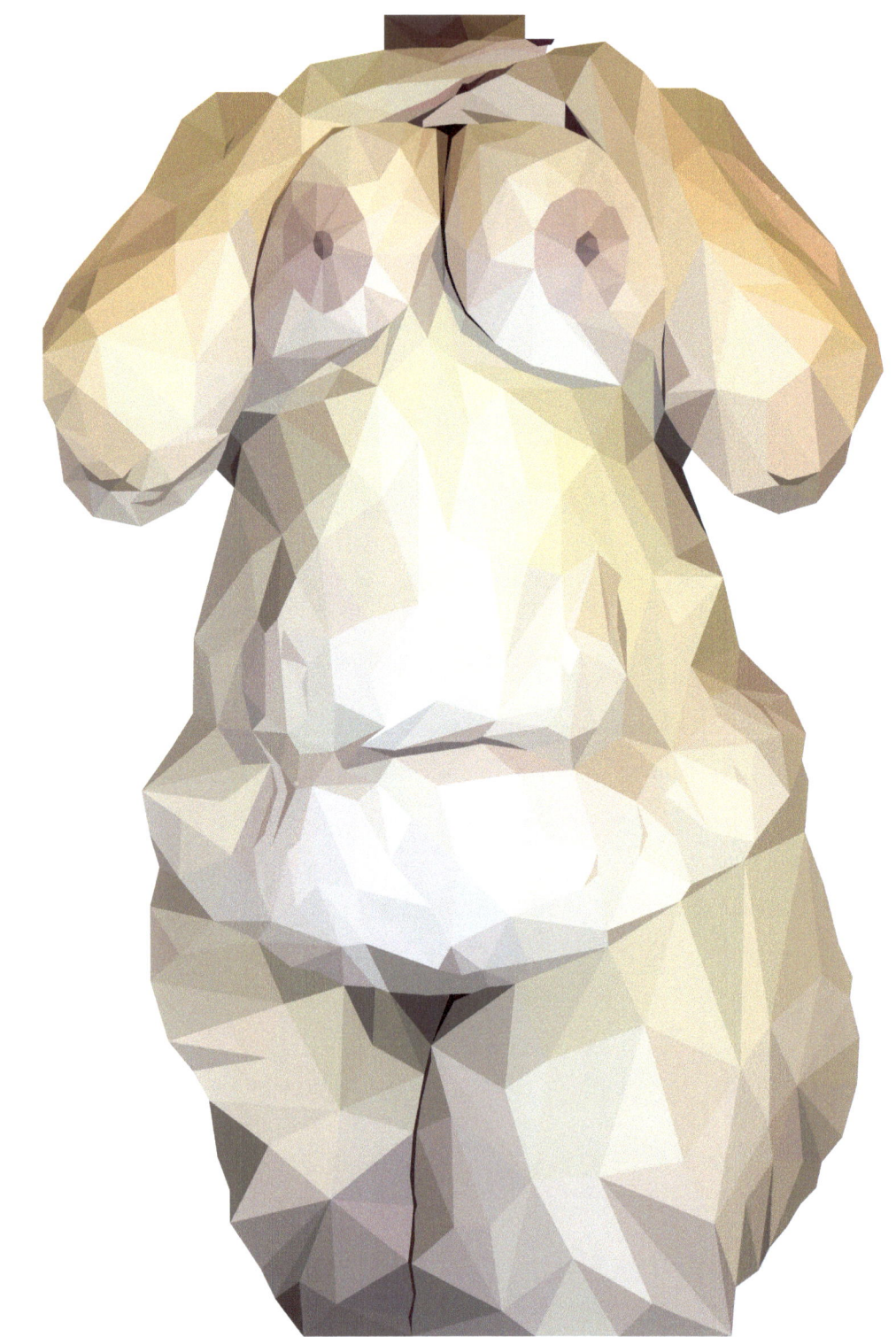

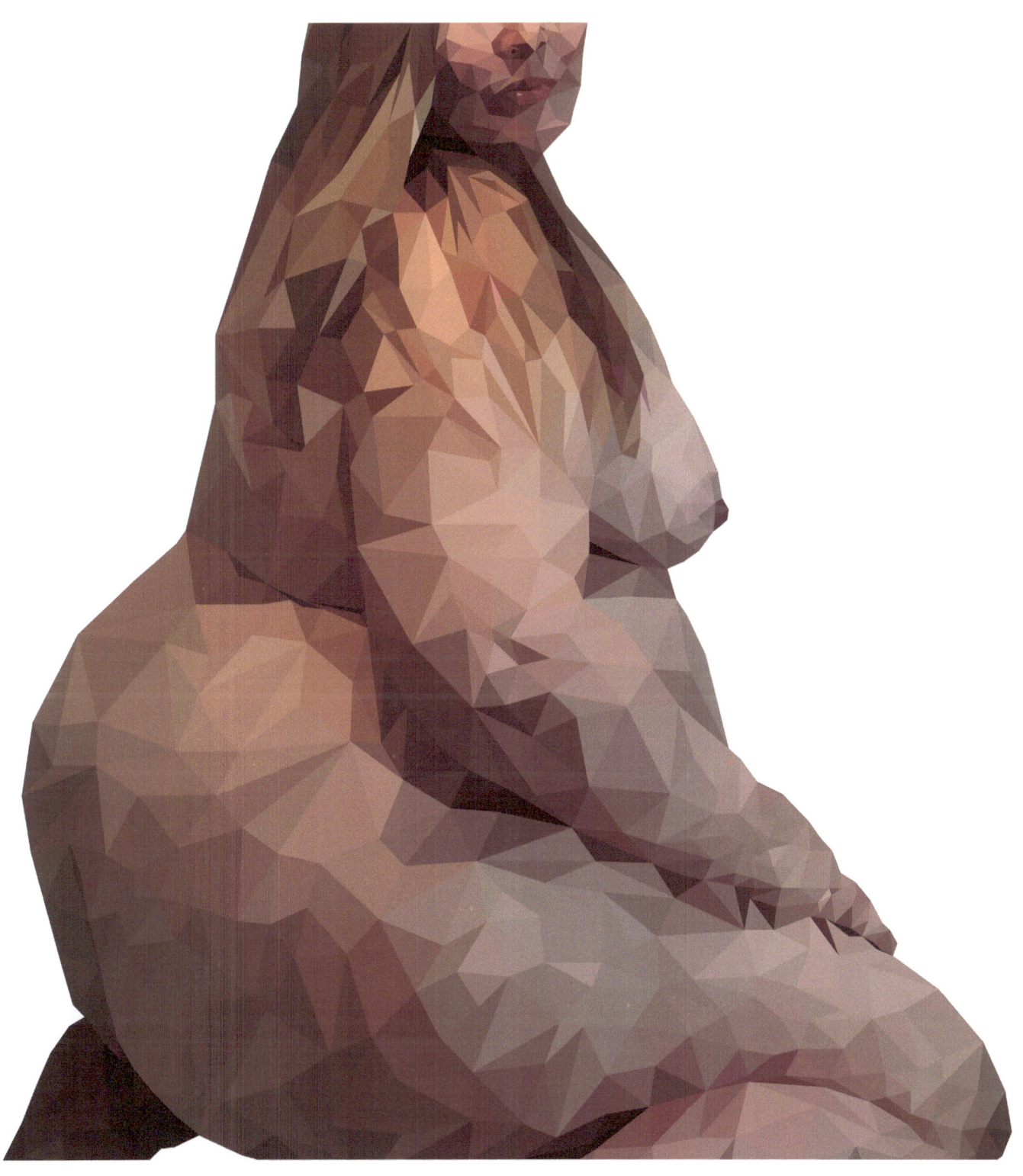

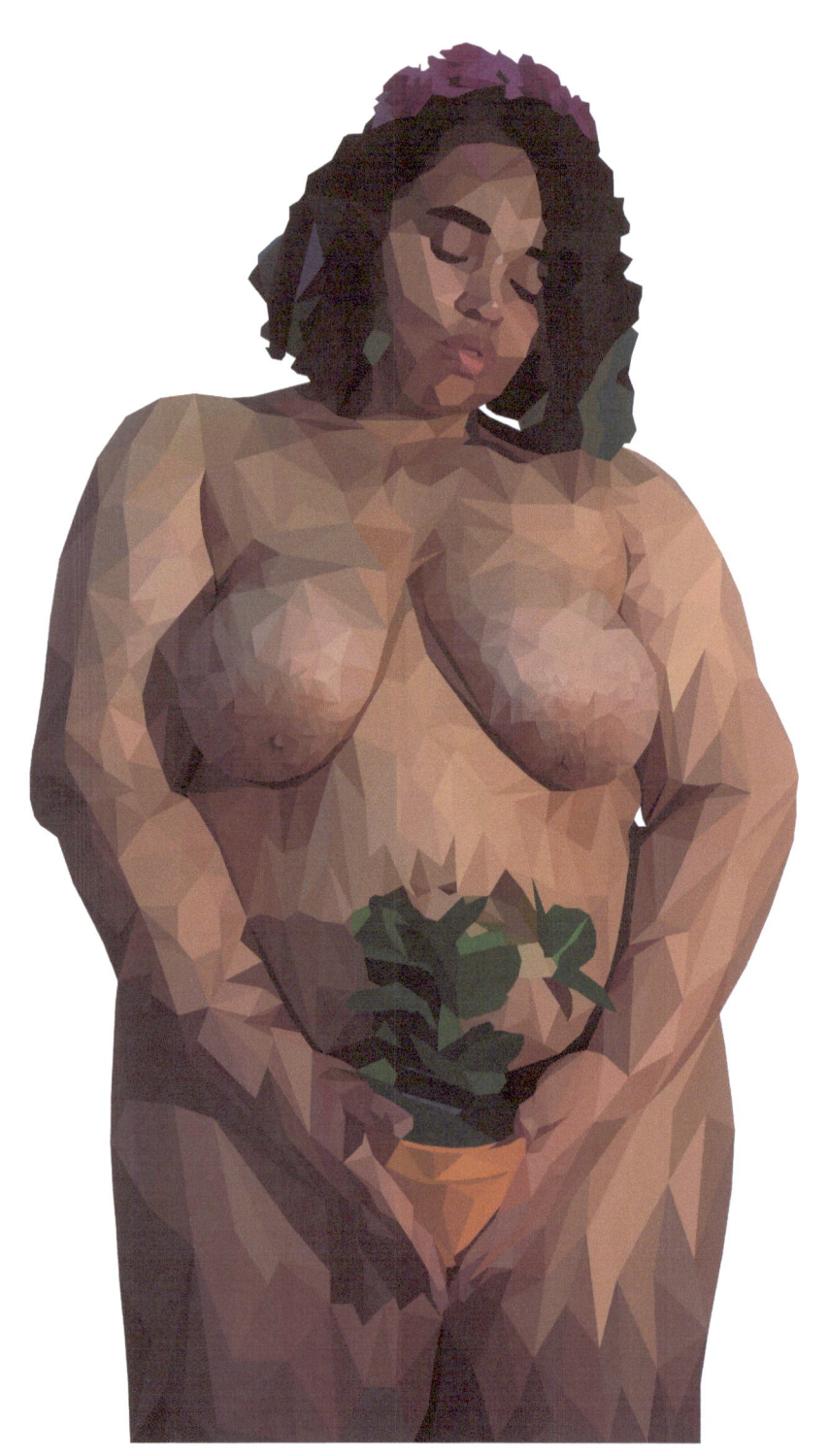

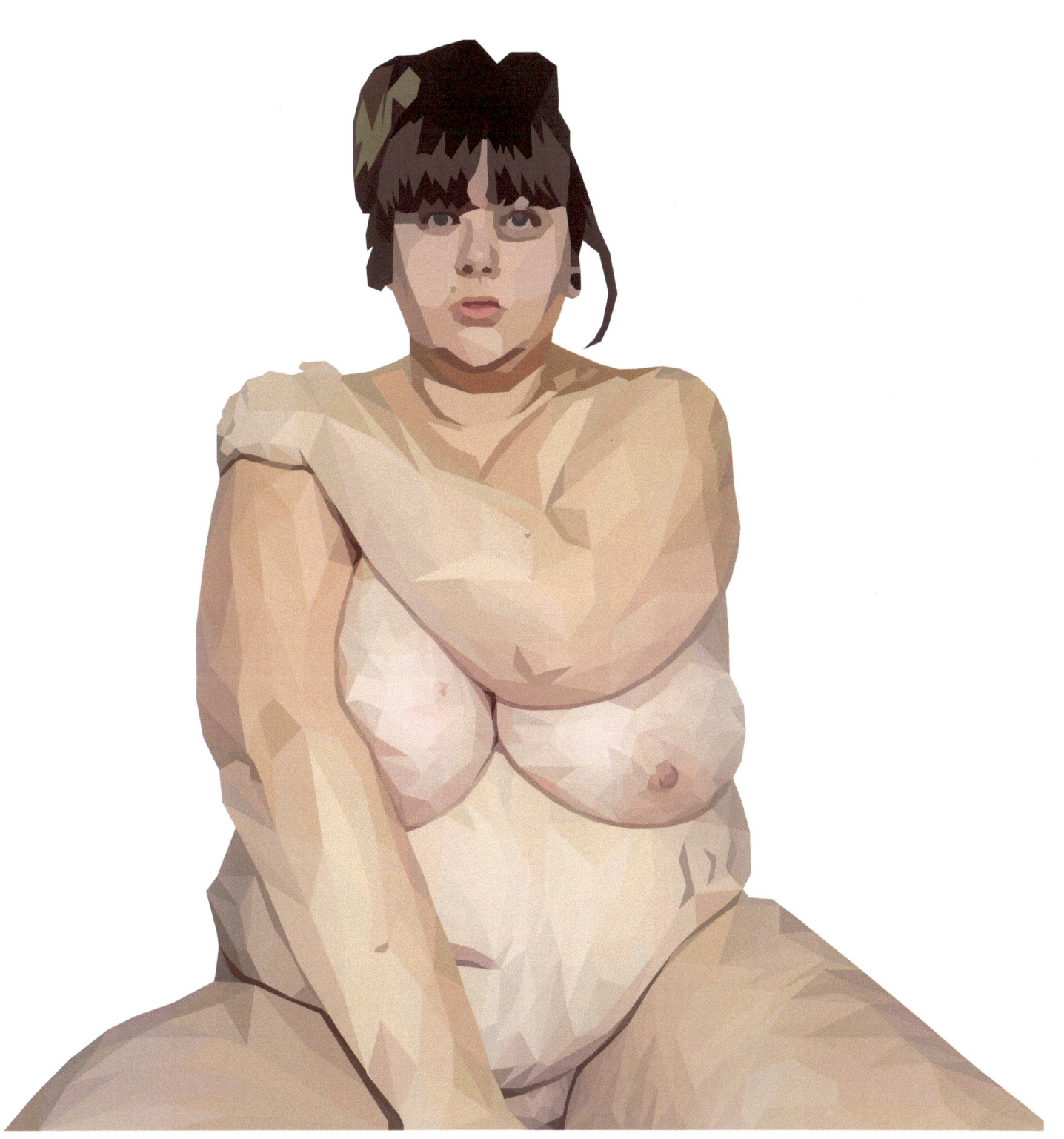

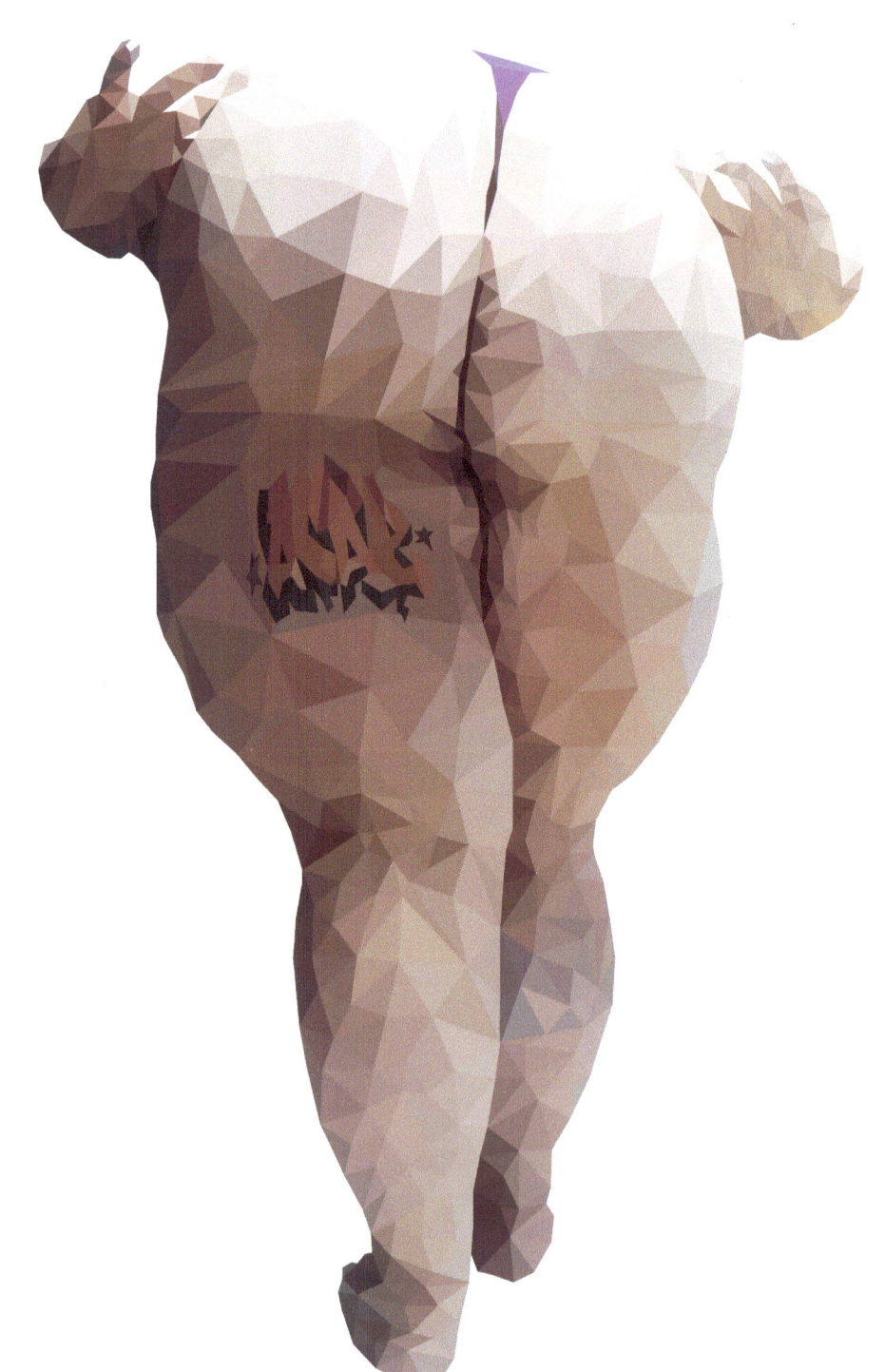

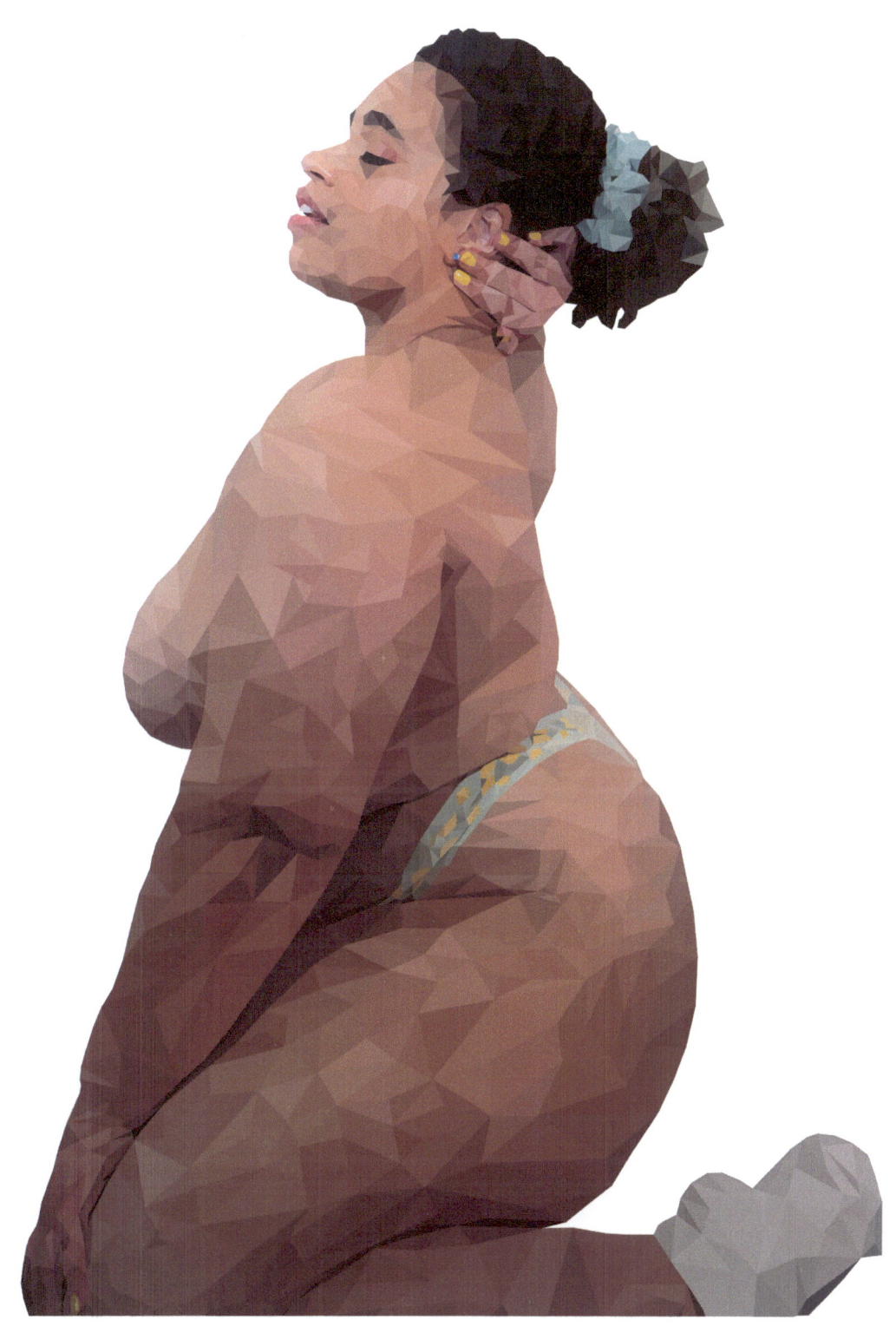

This body is the only one I've ever had. I remember it before cellulite and stretch marks. I don't remember when they came, but they did. I remember as my body began to spread, my hips a little wider, my breasts sagging a bit lower, and my stomach dancing with gravity, I started to notice the world. The world was seeing me in a way I hadn't noticed before. People were meaner, men were creepier, friends were isolating me, and adults were constantly judging me. I didn't know what I had done so wrong, I just knew my belly got softer and my body seemed more decorated with "flaws". That my jeans were 2 sizes bigger and movie seats got smaller and more uncomfortable. Through all this I never felt ugly or unwelcome in my own company. I knew my heart and I knew my joy. I was funny and attractive and smart. My ambitions were unmatched and boy was I clever. I thought, "if I want this thing/person/experience, I'm gonna go get it." But suddenly, I was reminded at every turn that my body was a barrier. I was perfect for being fetishized but never for loving. Perfect for training and welcoming new hires at work but never for promotions and company representation. I became sex and not sexy. I felt like the comedian but more often than not, was the joke. I was the aggressor when my feelings were hurt and the talking point, when I only wanted to be in the audience.

When you have a fat body, the world chooses which piece of you is the good piece for the moment. Socially it is about which part of you they can tolerate today. Professionally it is about which piece of you is allowed to exist so you don't scare anyone off. Sexually it is about how much abuse you can handle in exchange for pieces of intimacy. Romantically it is about your heart and how it loves, in spite of what your body looks like. A lifetime of "I don't care how you look, I love you anyway," from lovers who treat investing in you like overcoming an obstacle. Fat people become masters at knowing which piece of themselves is allowed to exist and which pieces they have to tuck away.

I decided some time ago to stand firm in my own fatness. I will often be the biggest in the space. I've lived through unique traumas because of my fatness; Unique relationship abuses because of my fatness. I'm always going to have a hard time buying clothes and going to amusement parks. BUT, I exist. And I deserve to exist in peace. This body, all bodies, should never be loved conditionally. I love me, even when no one else does. I praise me, even when the world is quiet about me. I've mastered being fat in pieces, but I realize now that I want to be fat in peace. And I'm not asking permission anymore. You shouldn't either.

Words by Diamond Wynn

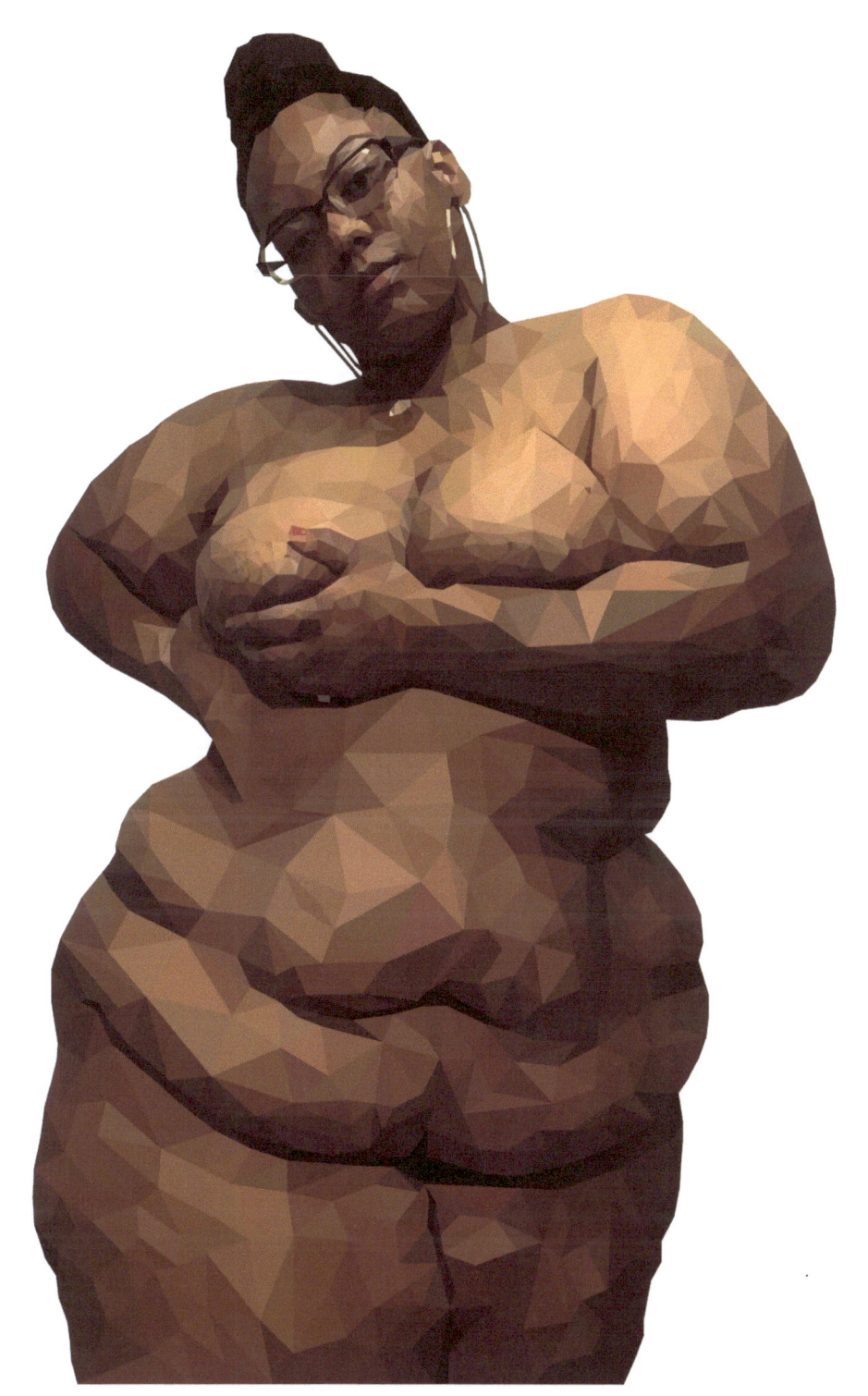

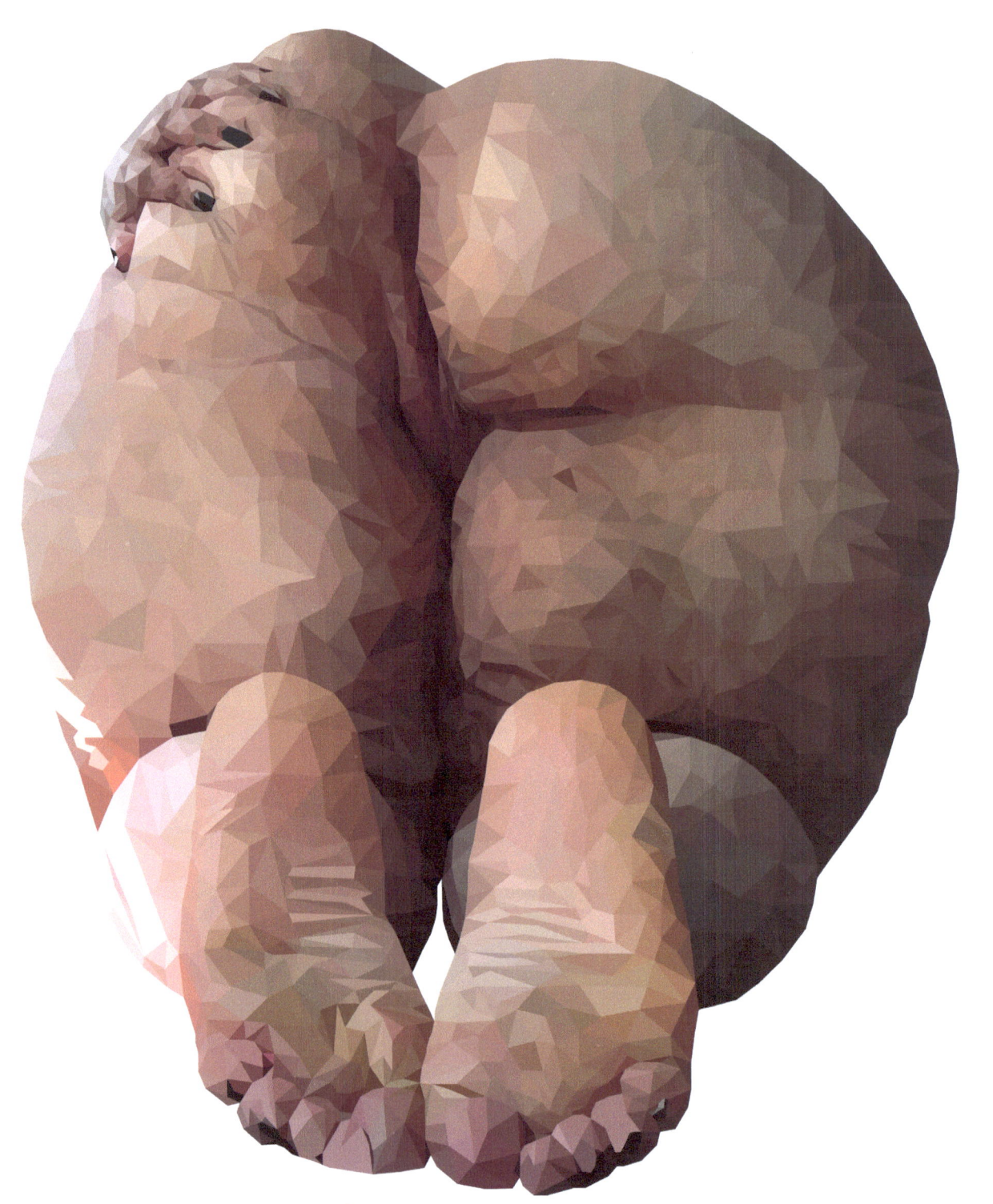

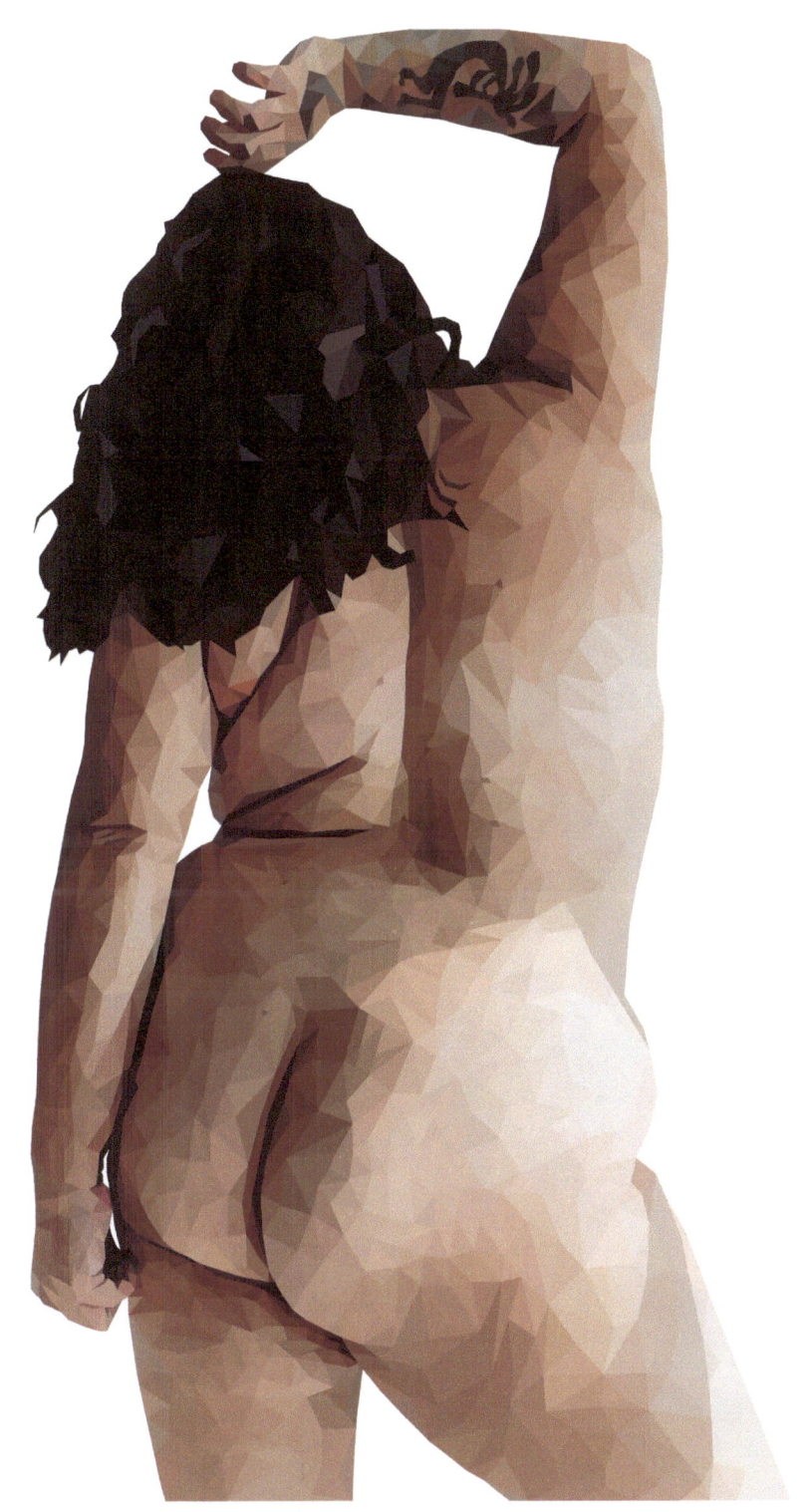

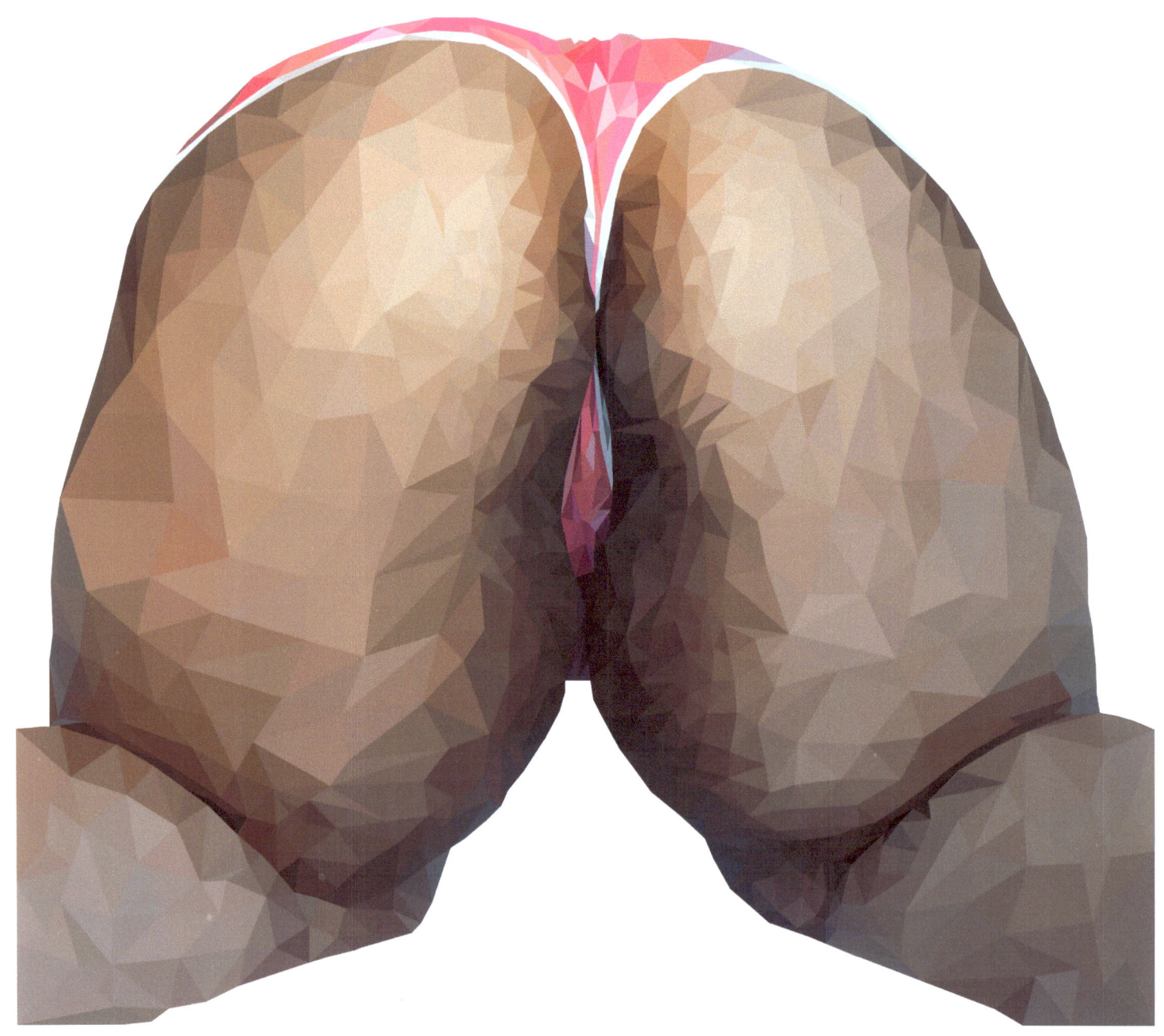

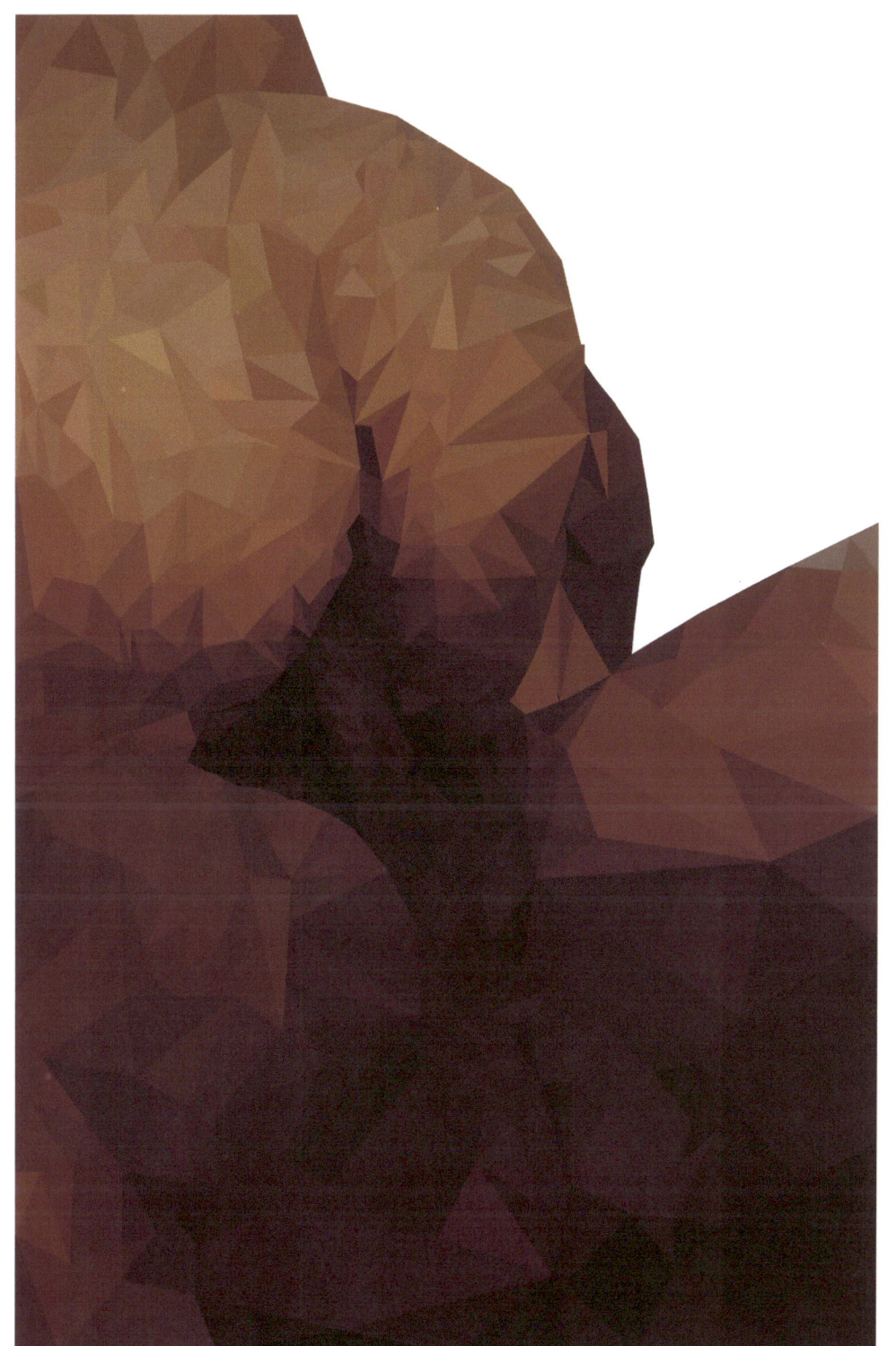

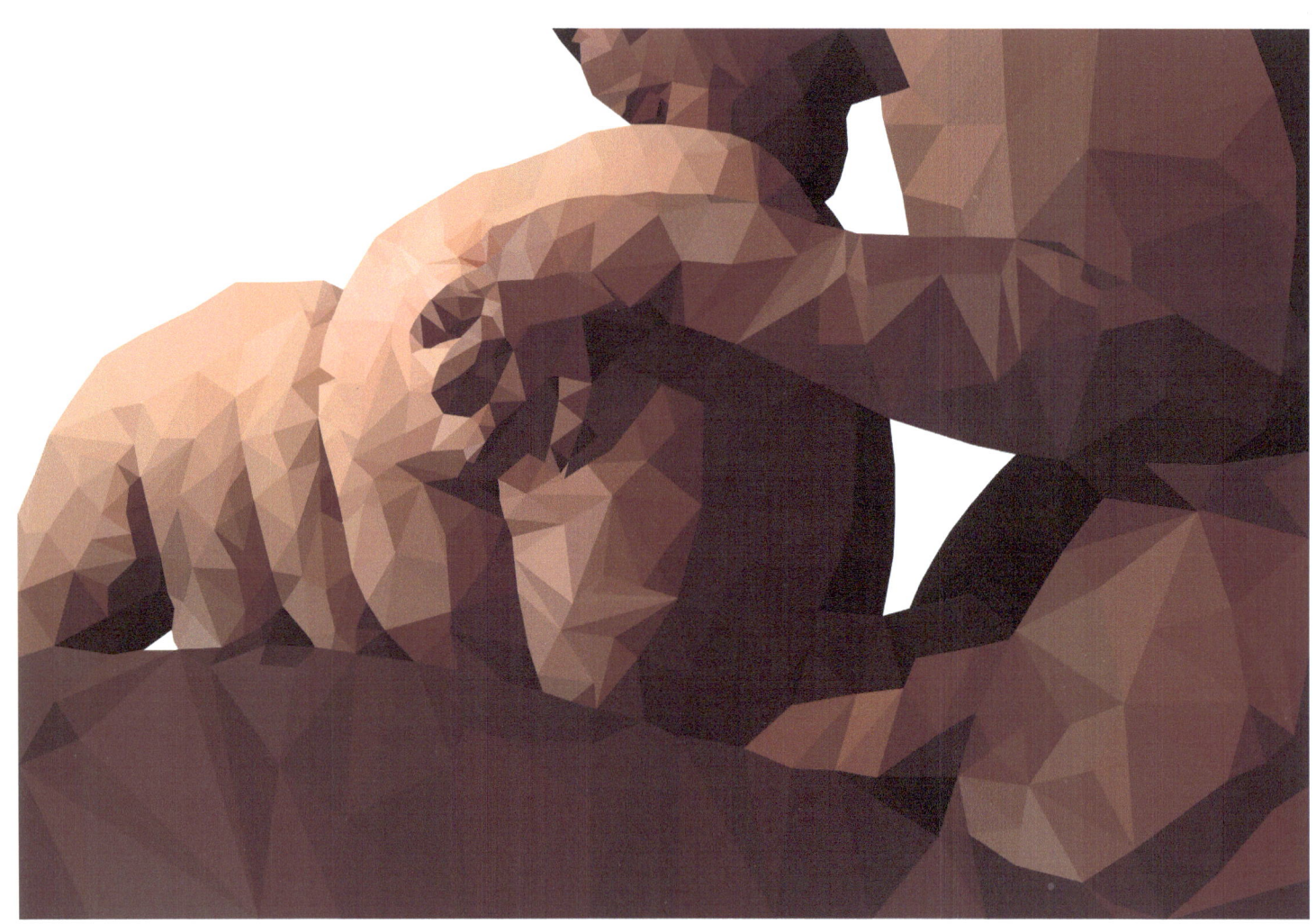

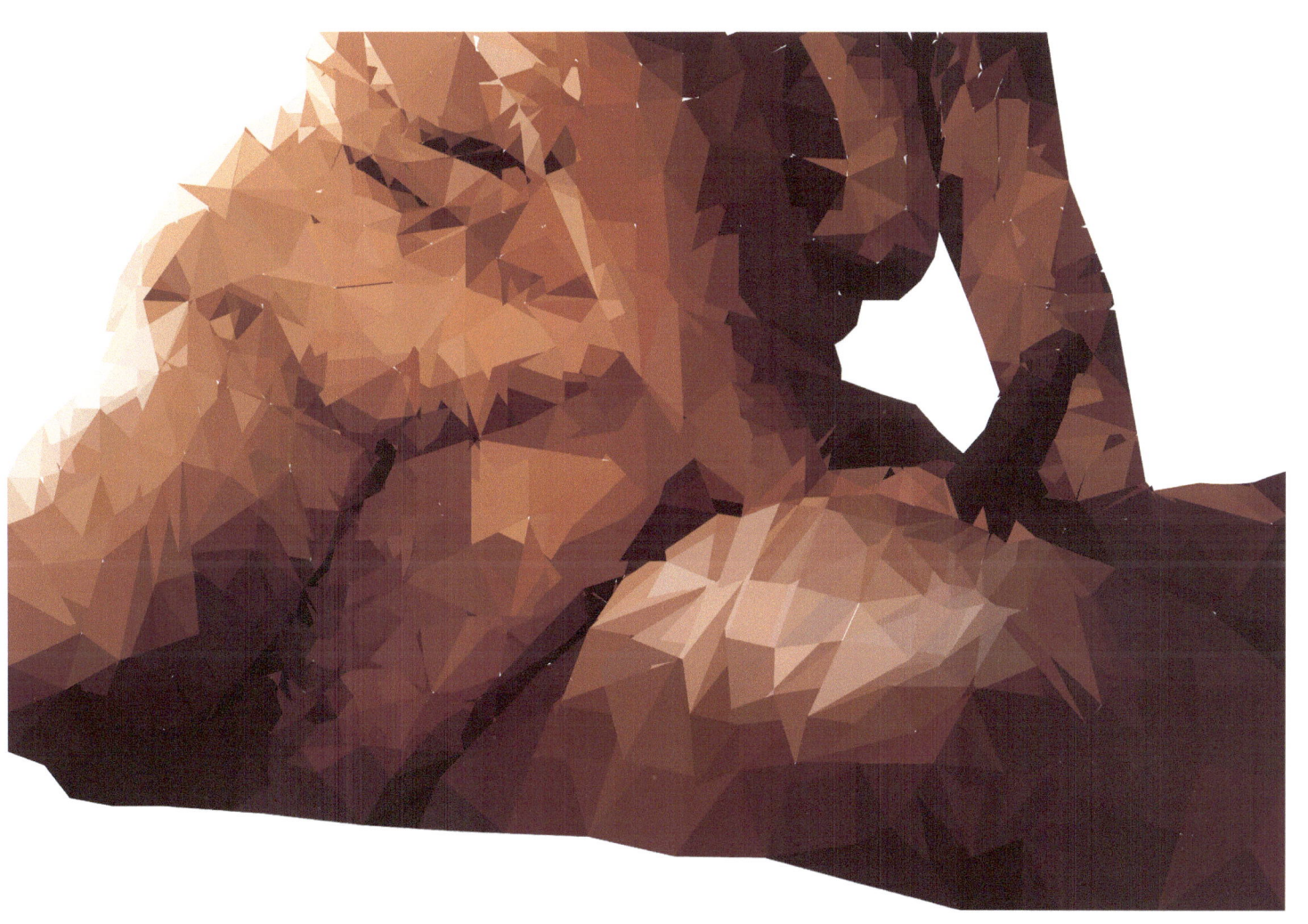

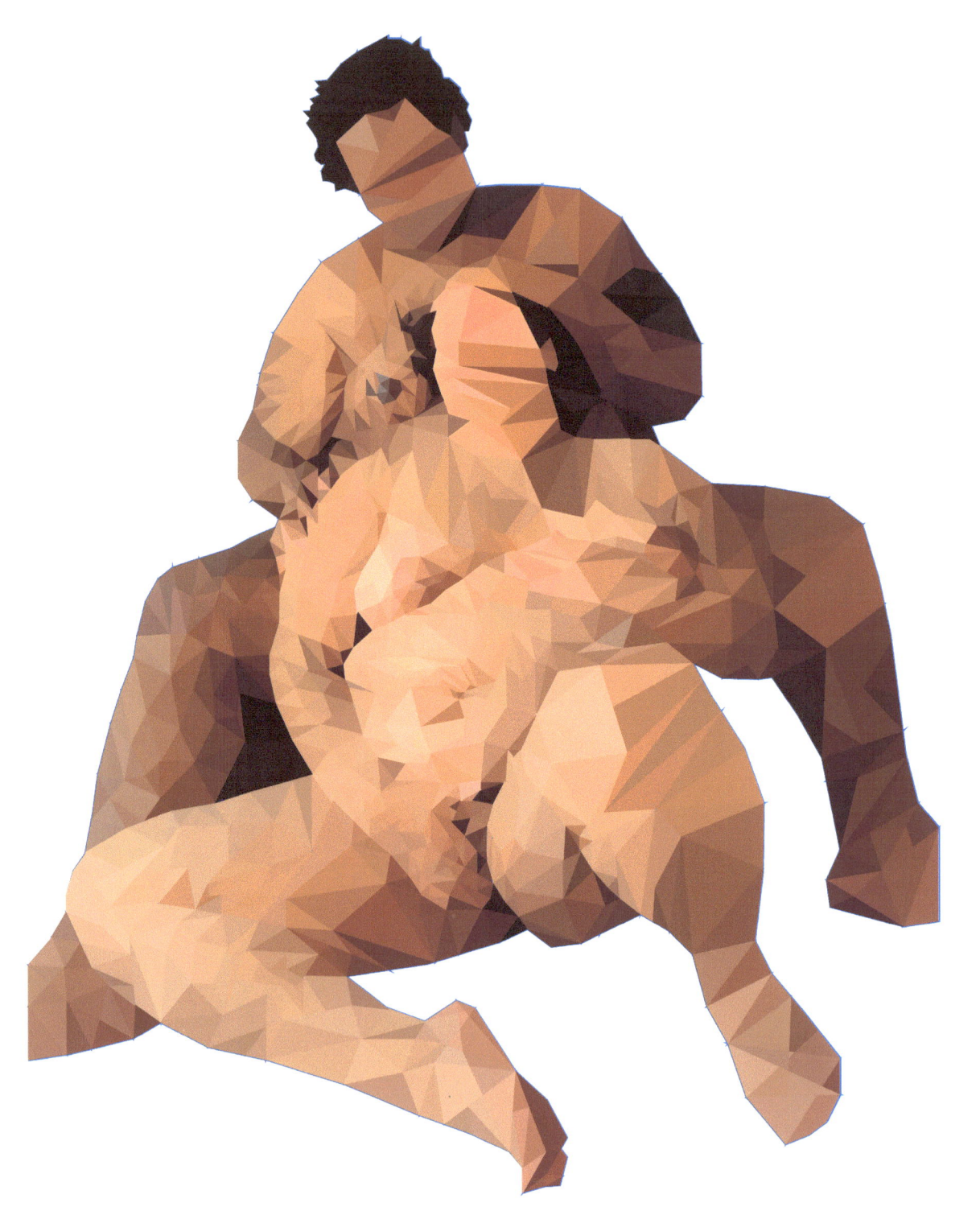

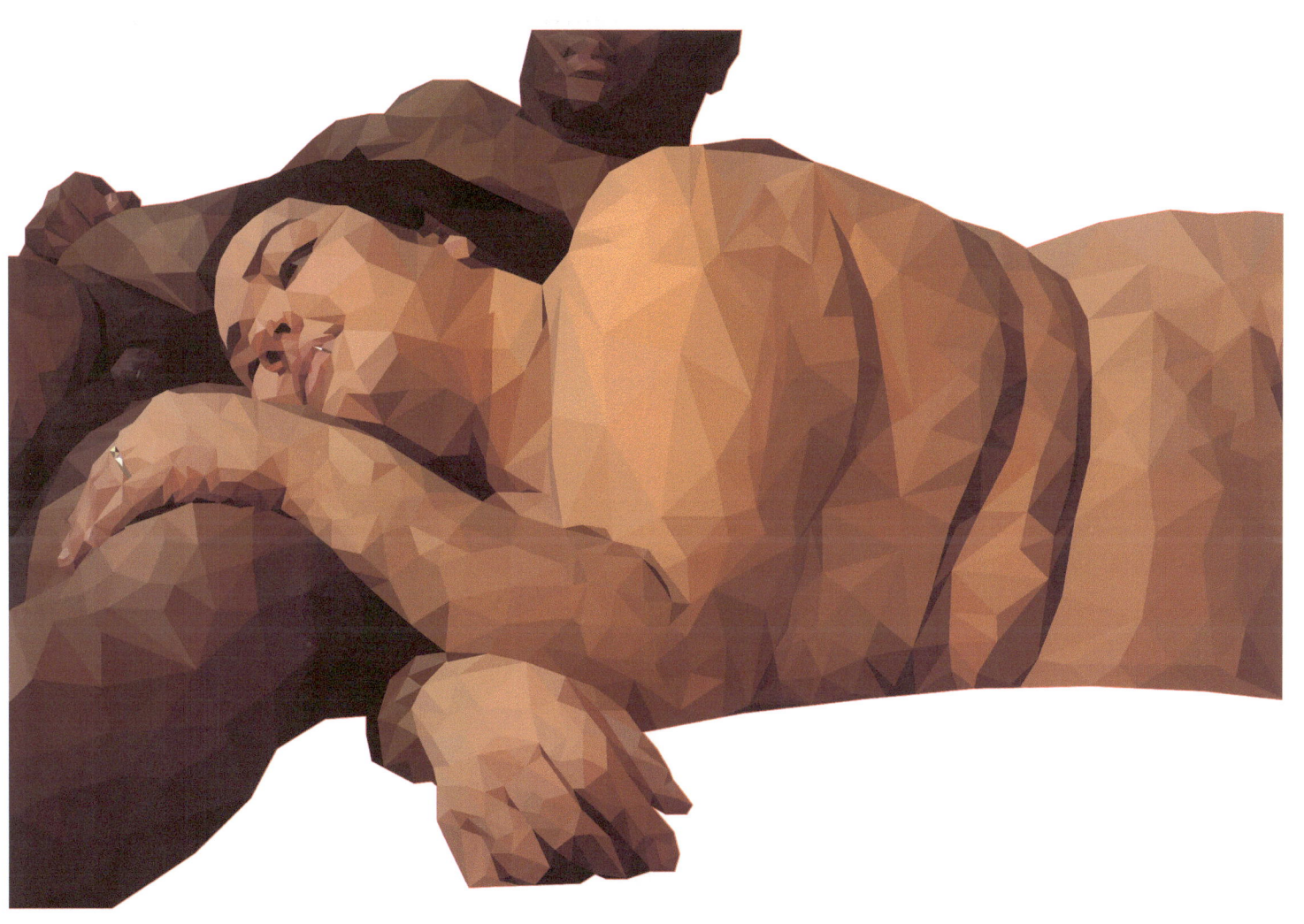

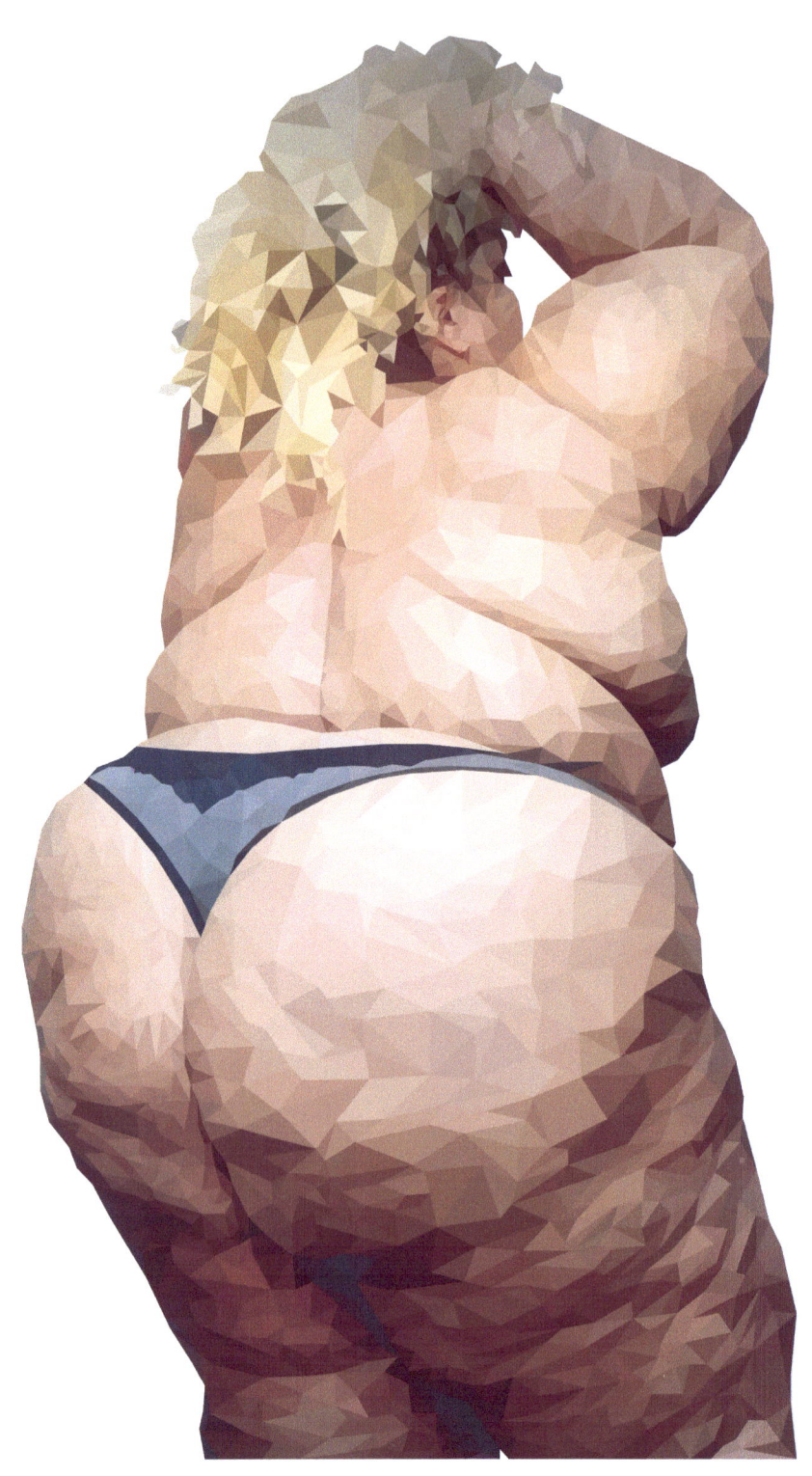

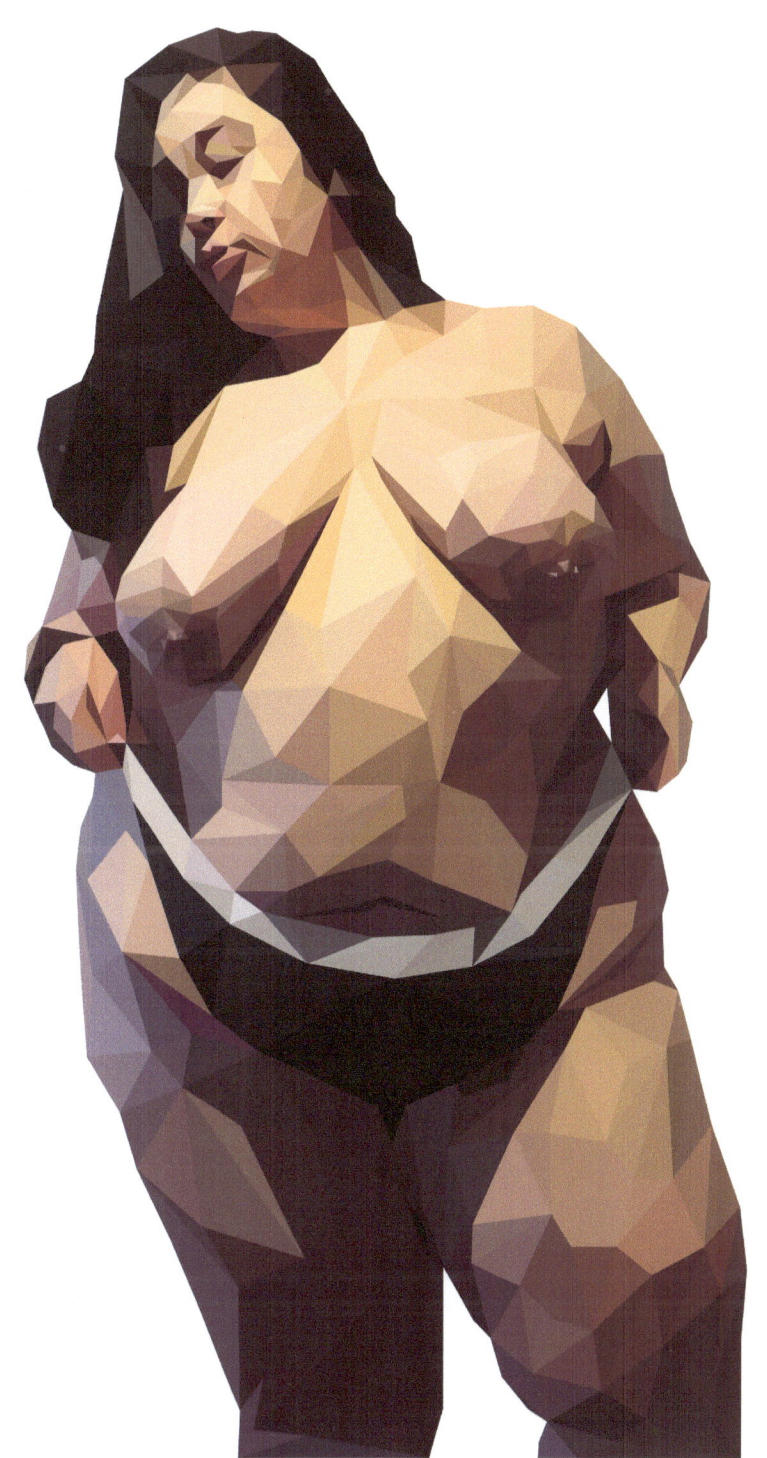

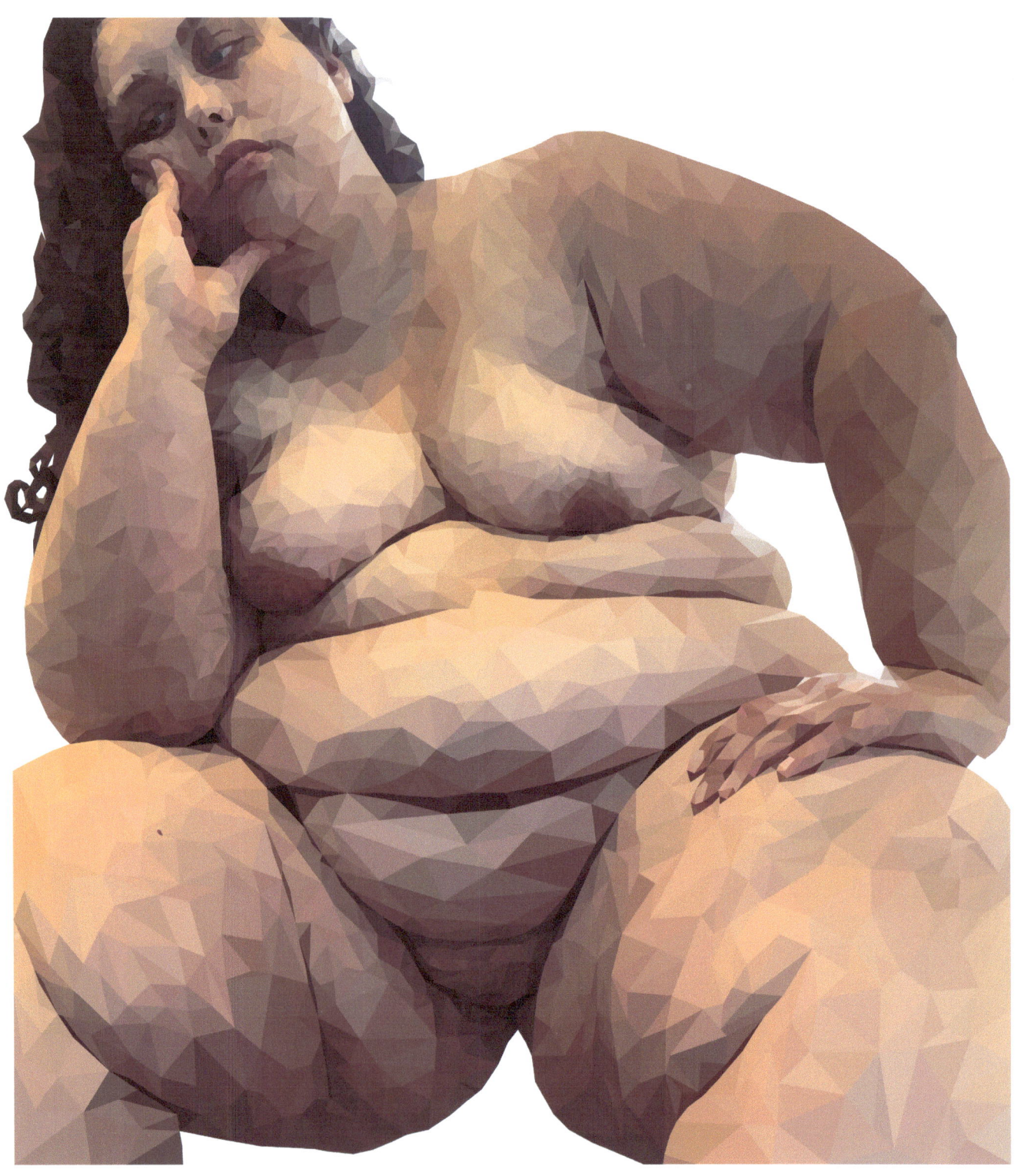

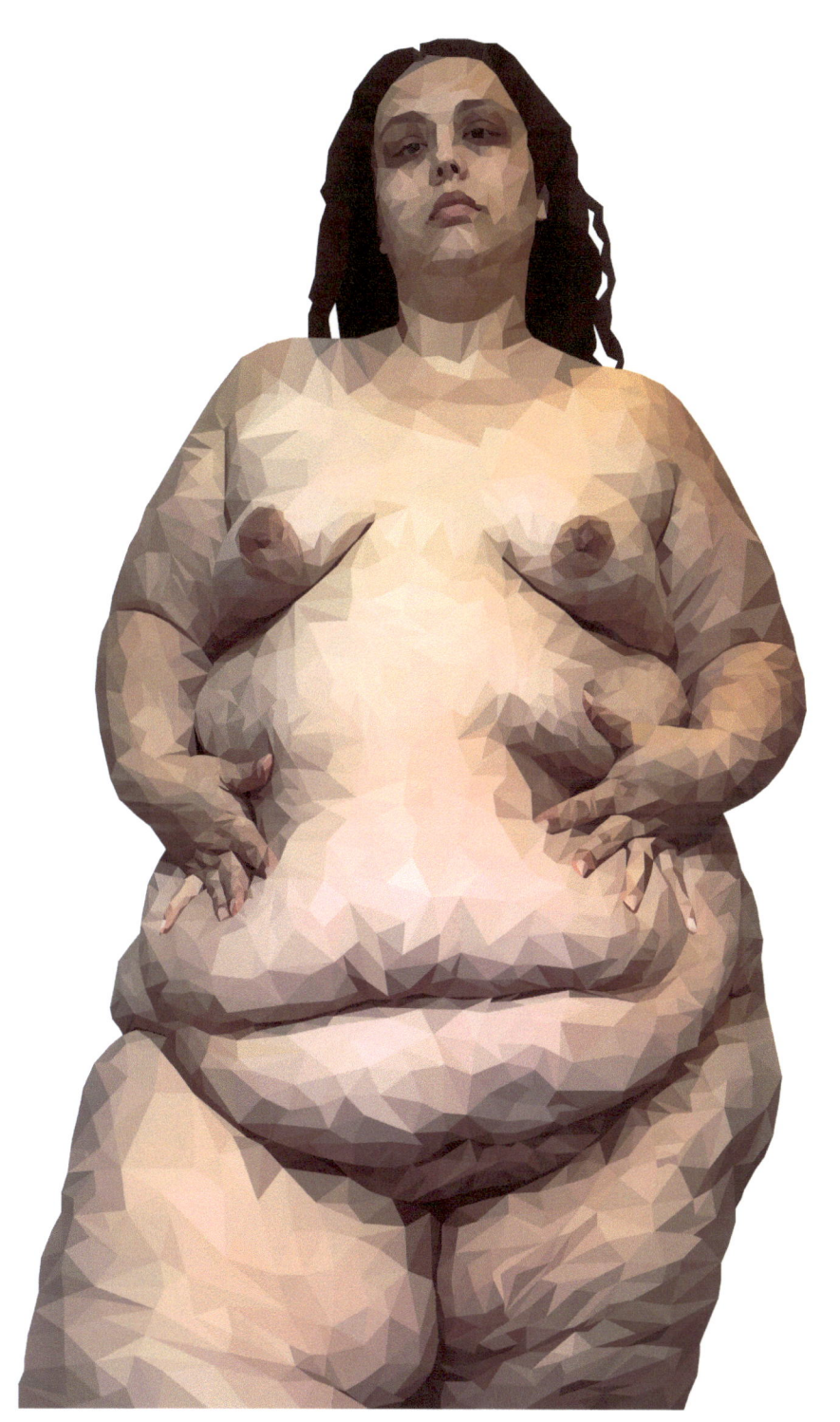

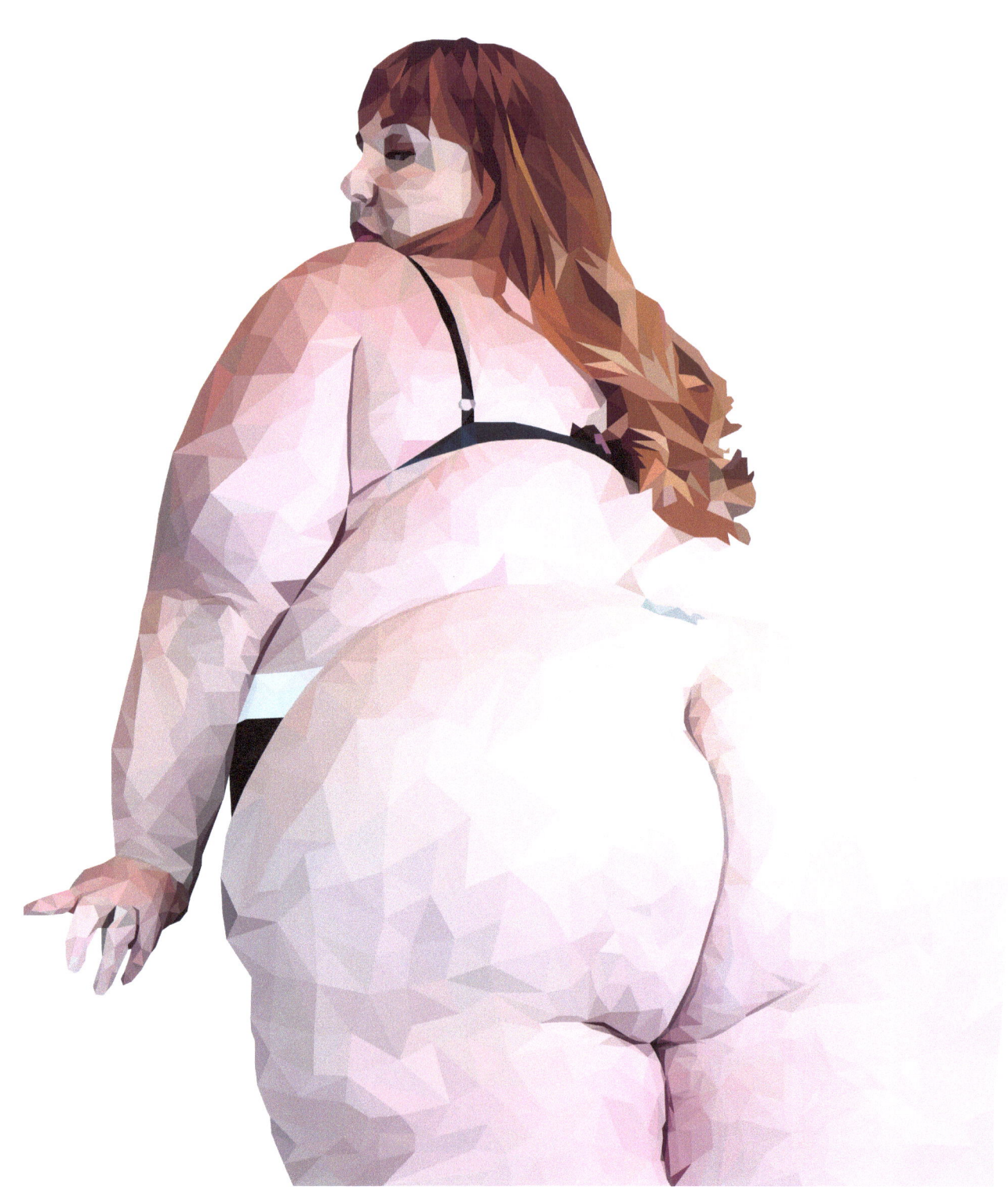

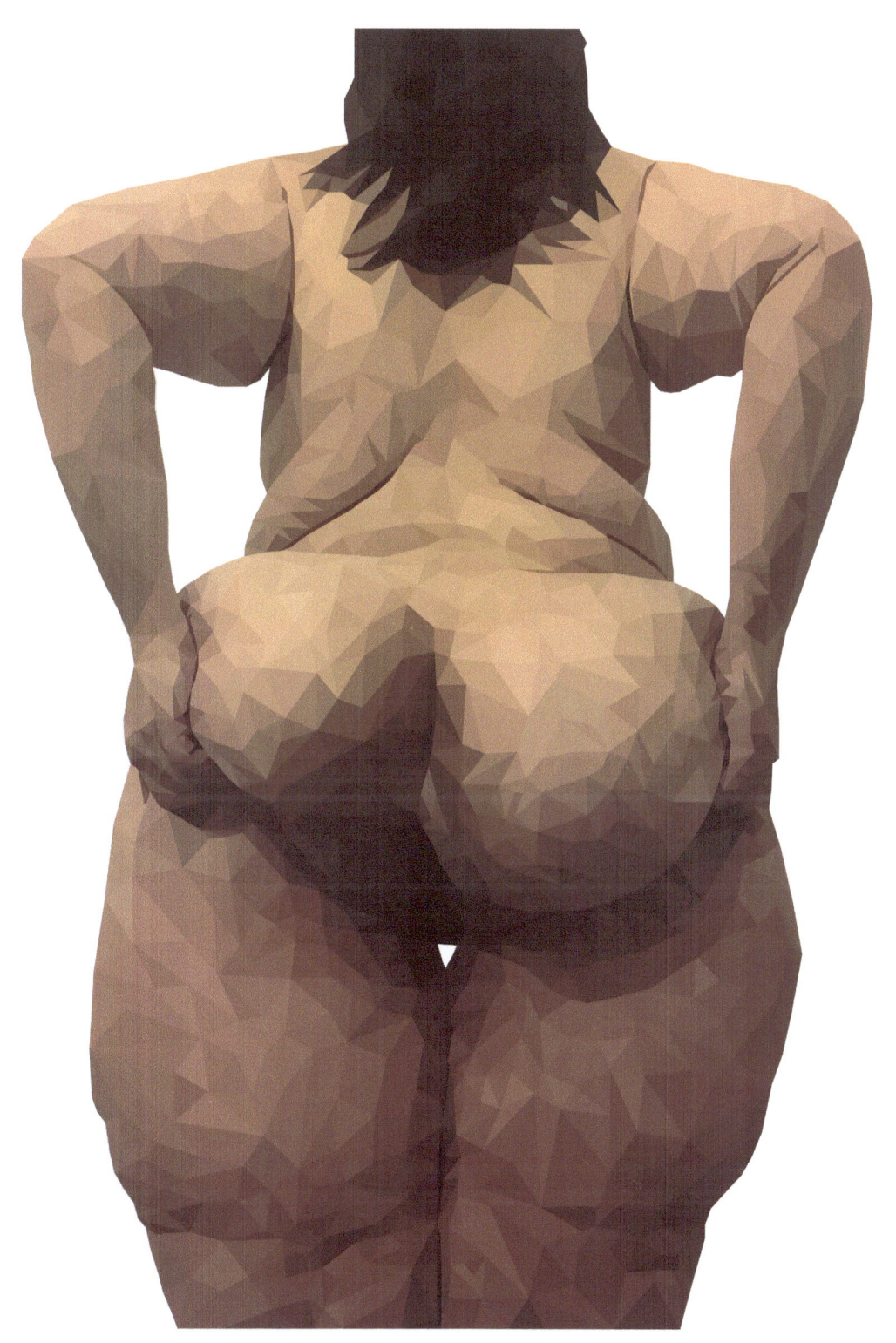

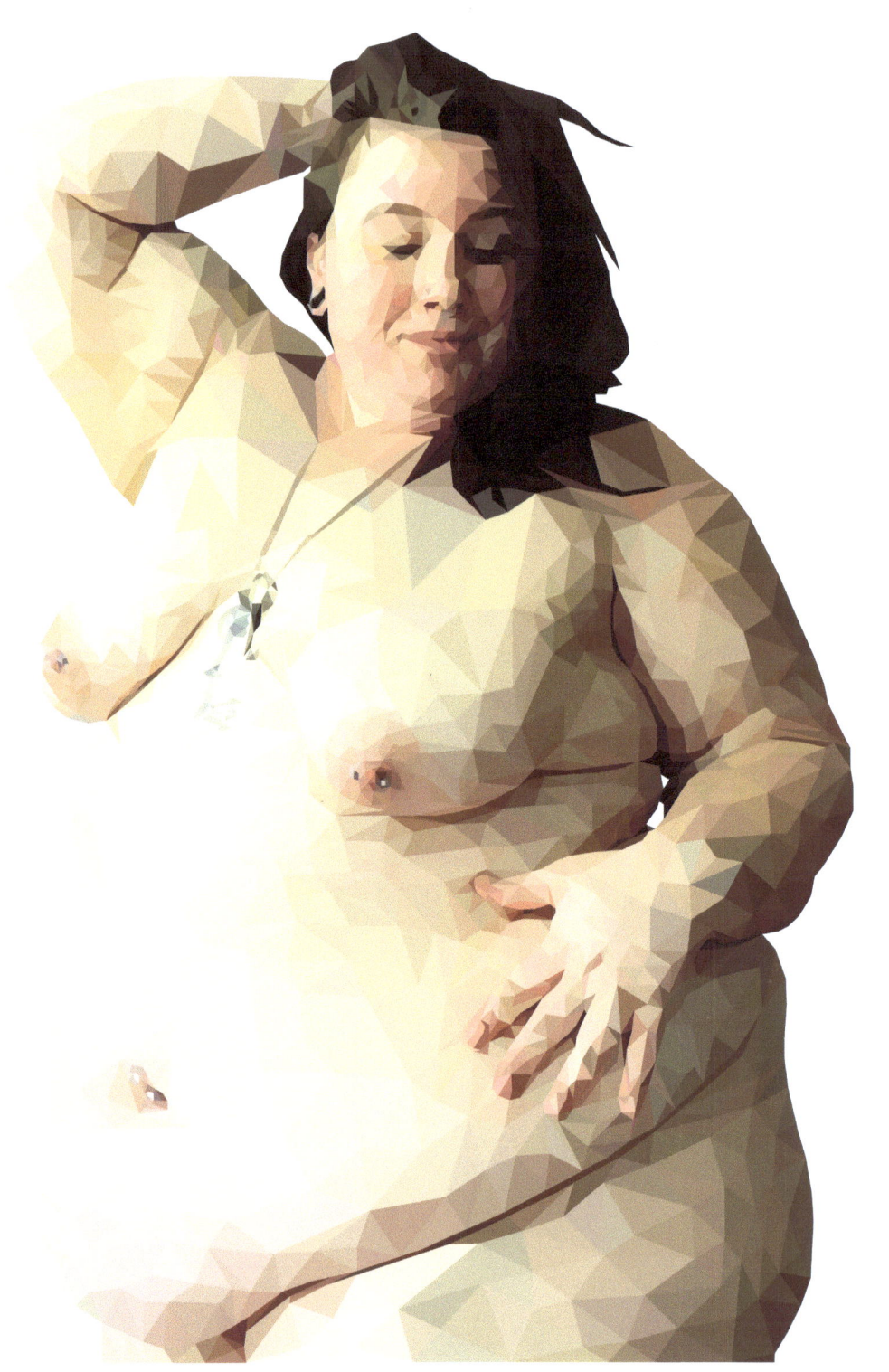

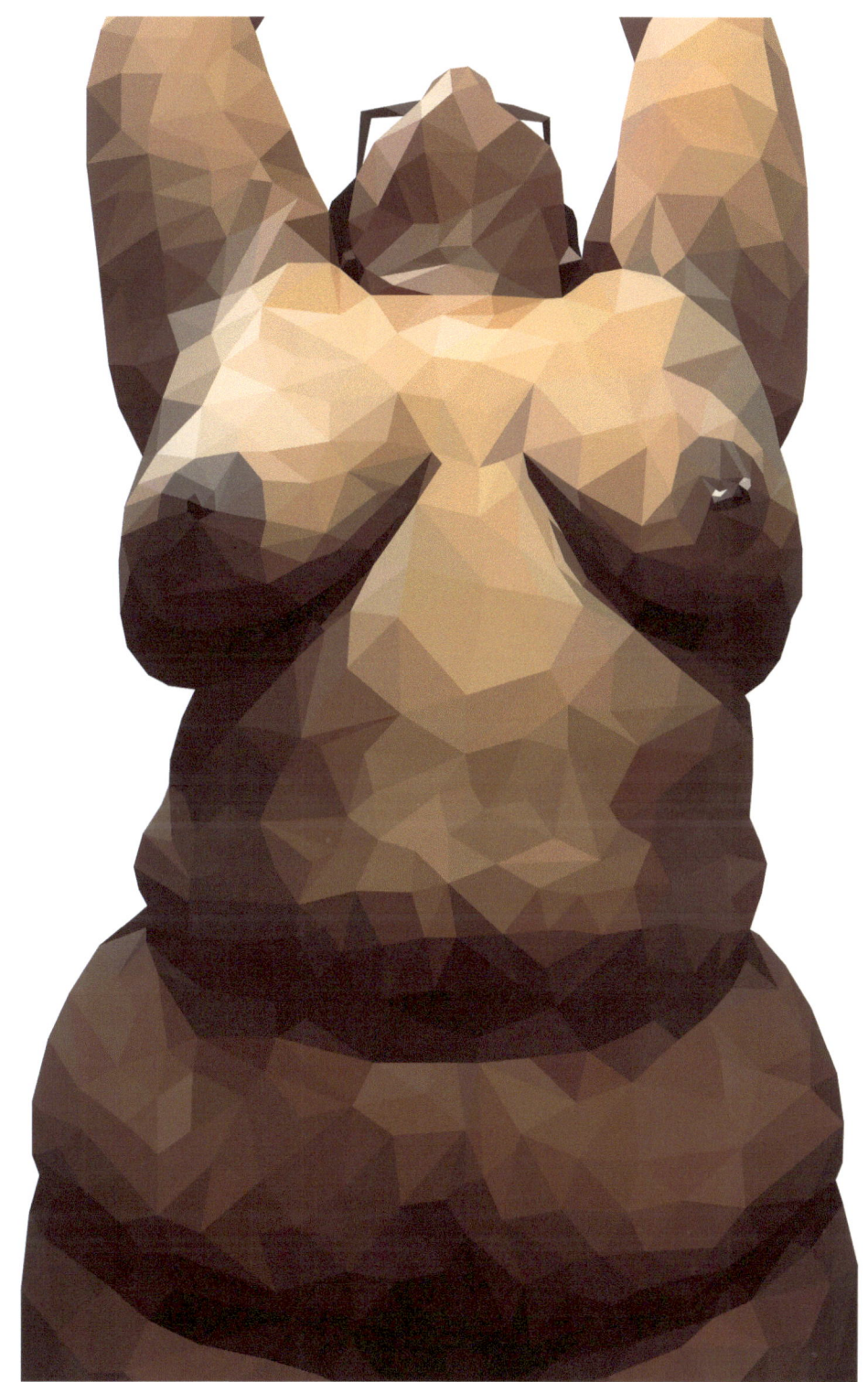

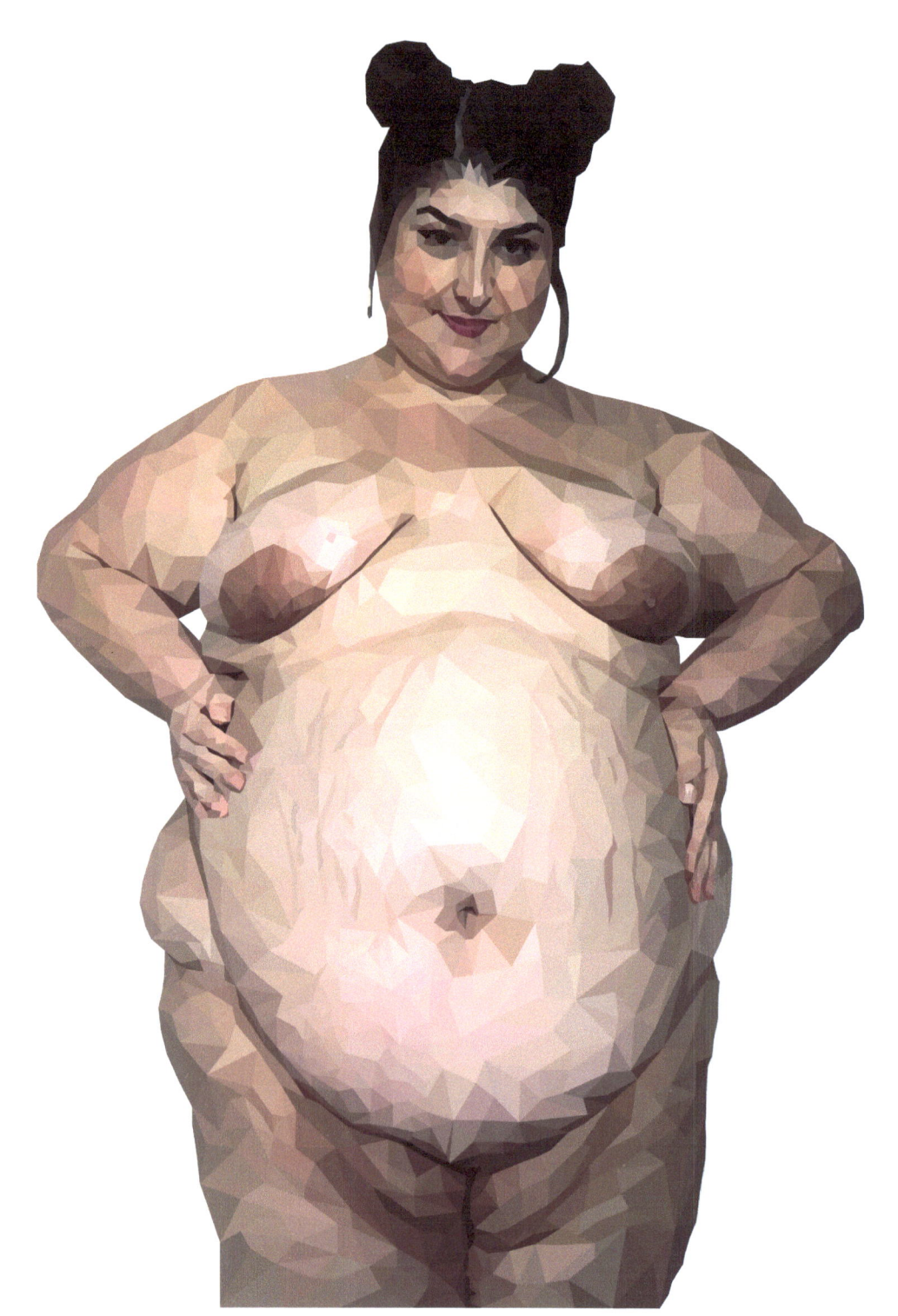

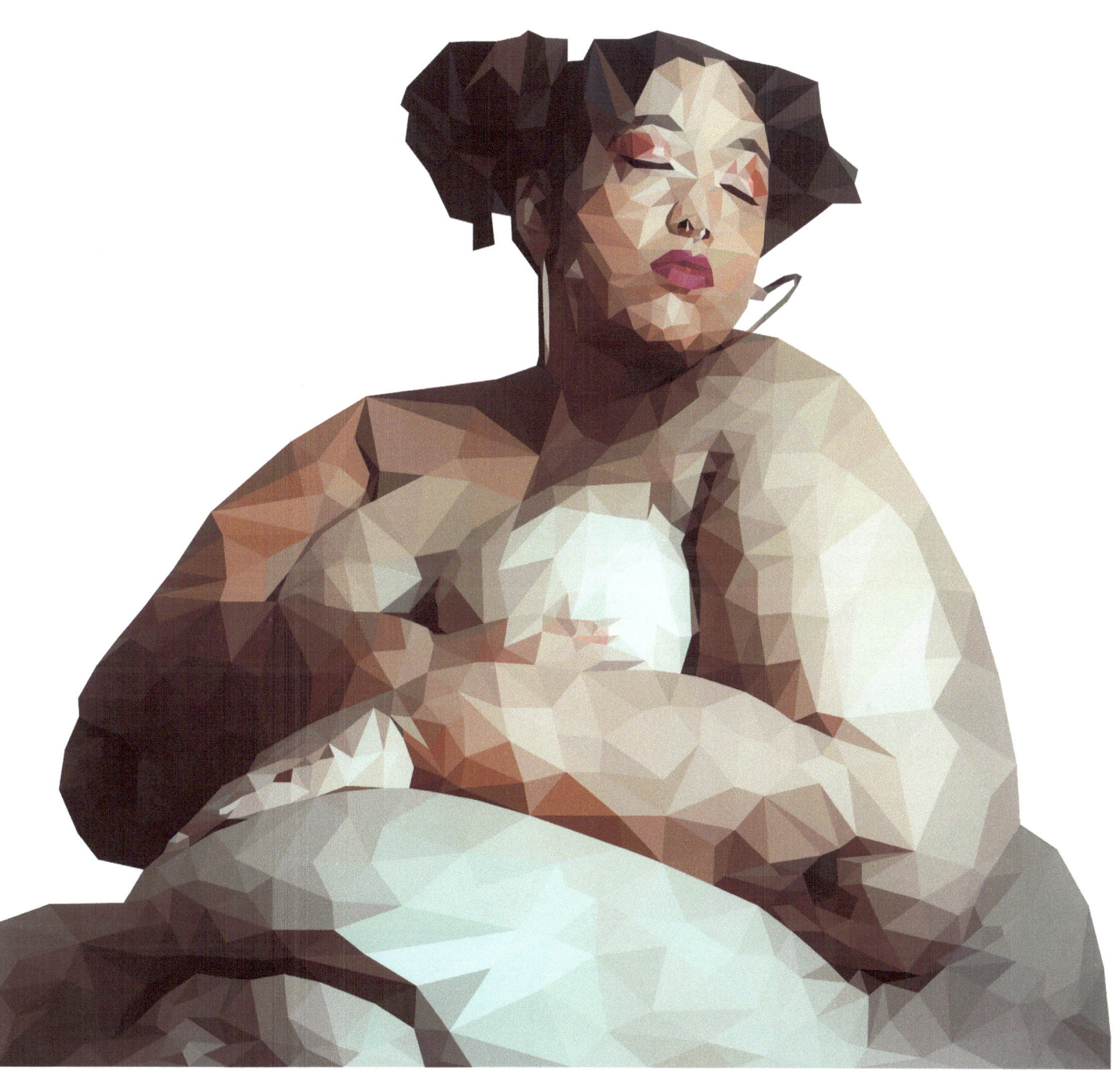

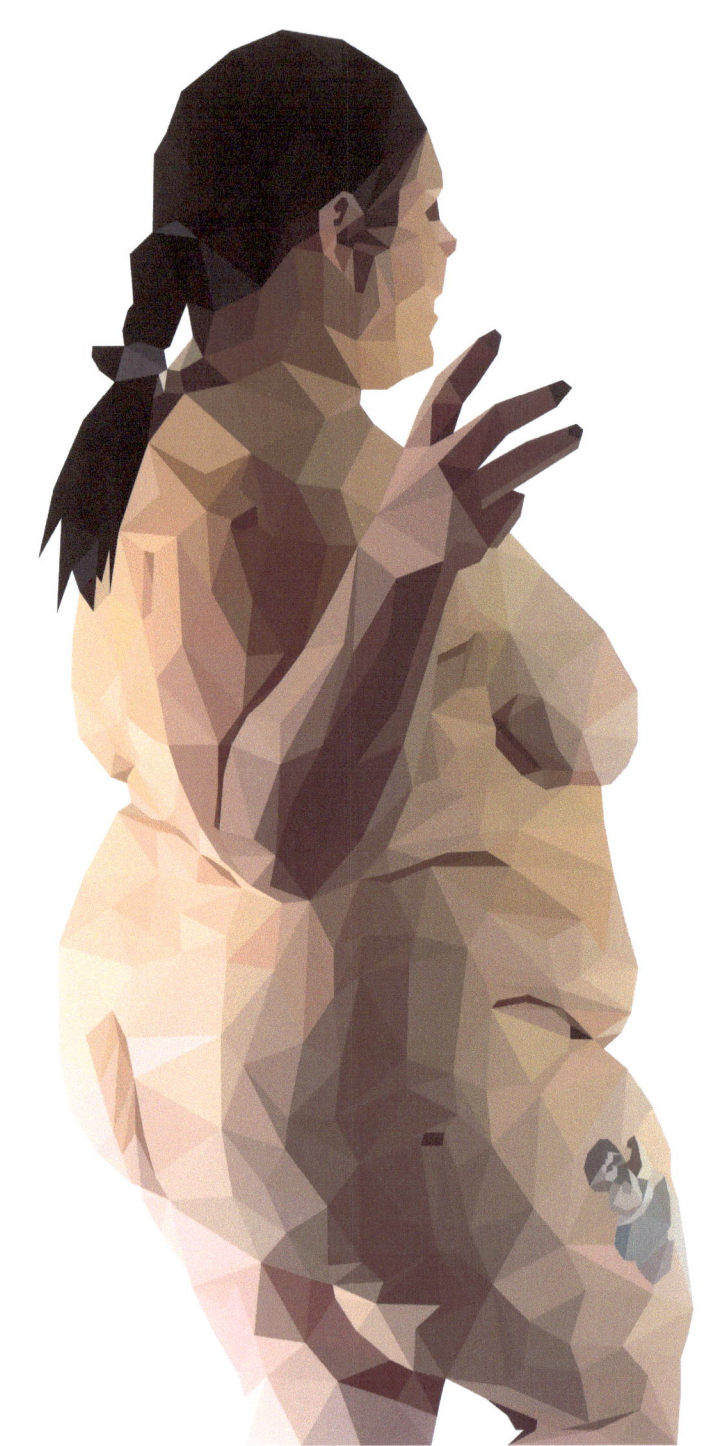

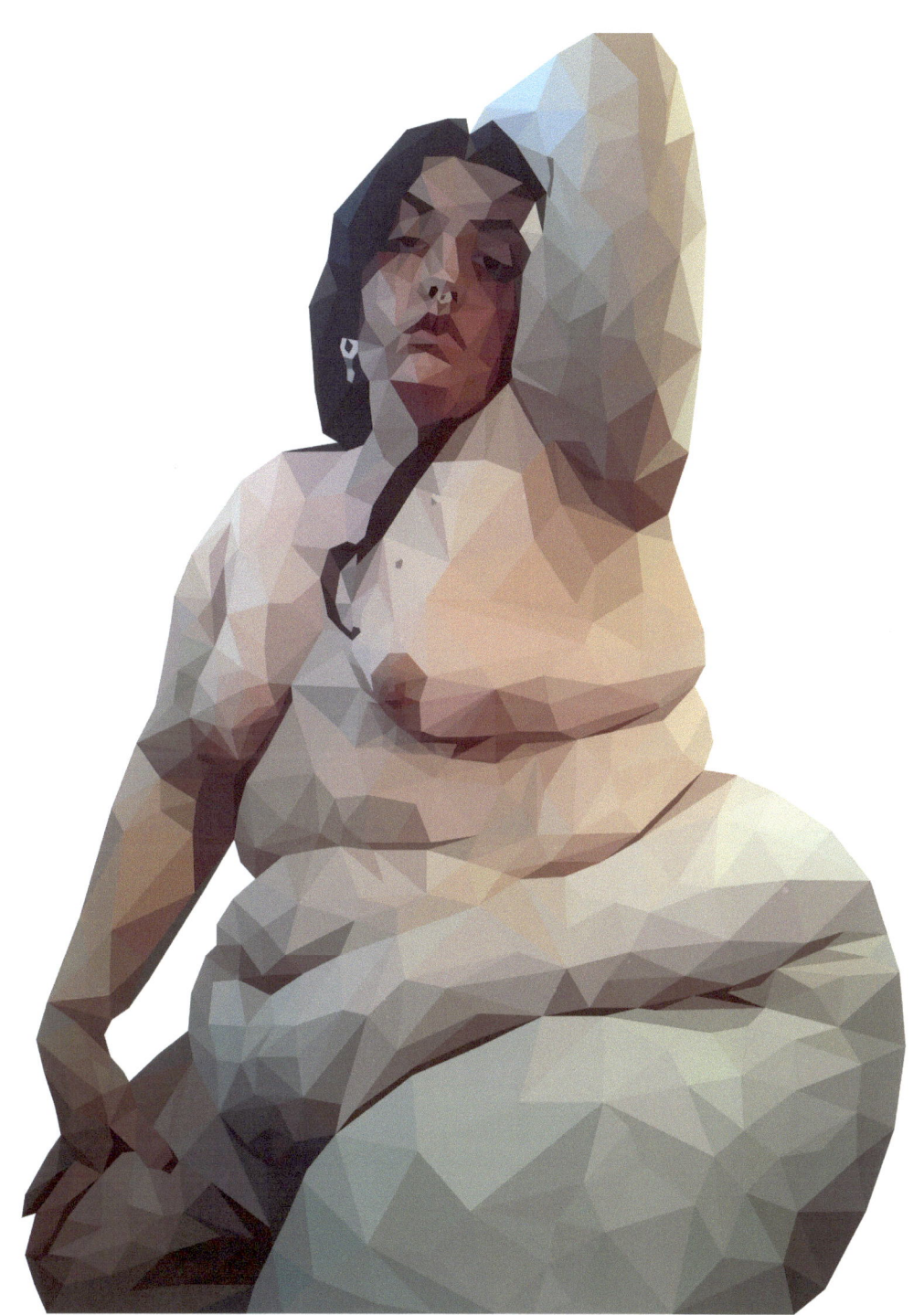

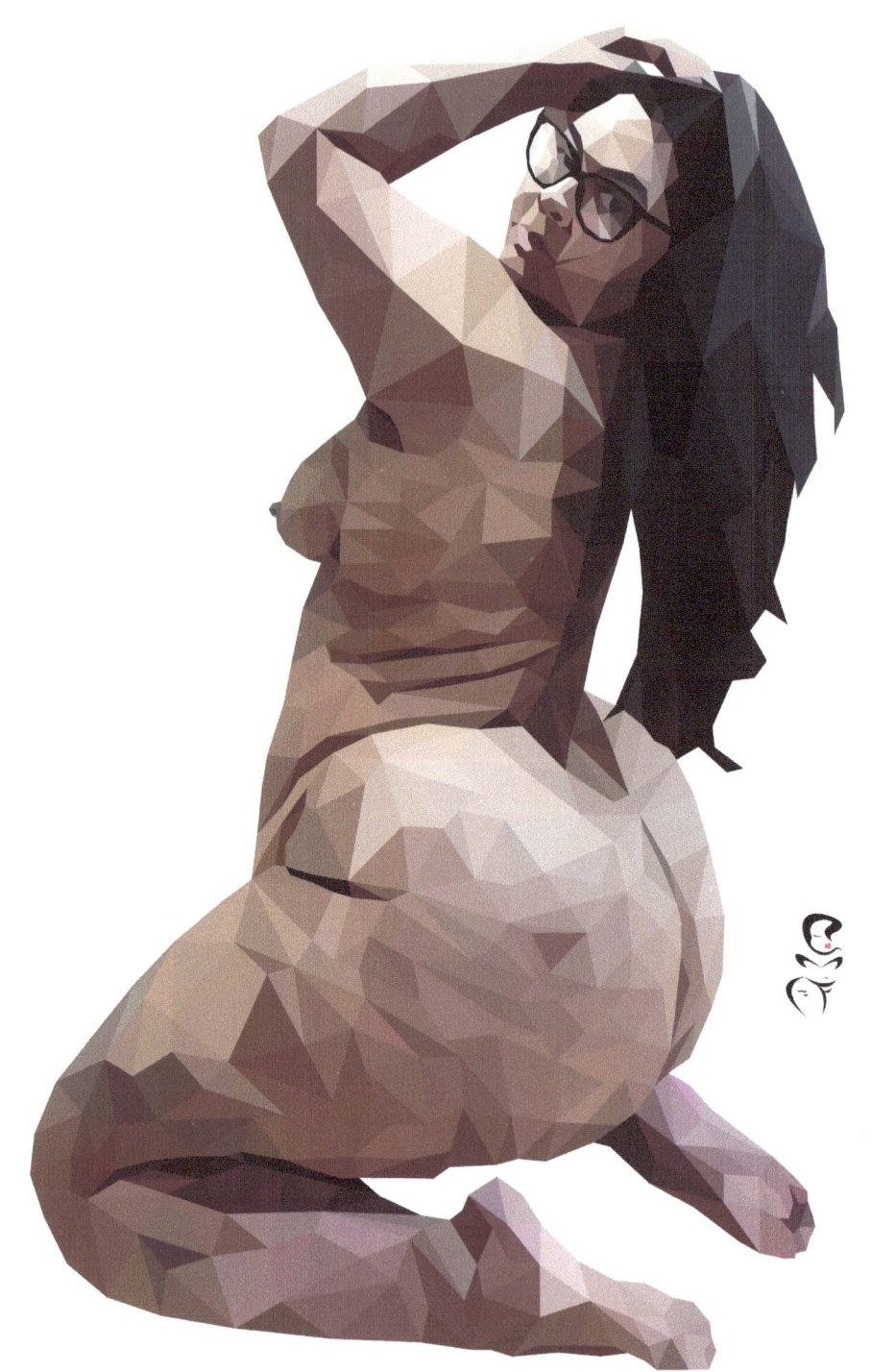

Special Thanks

To all of you who participated in this project,
You are flawless.

Highness Noire	@loveadipose
Rebecca Snagg	@officialanyaithesaiyan
Adele	Vivienne Rose
KiKi	Nicole Wilmoth
@chefdiamante	Ambyr Rincon
Chloe Venom	Cynthia Keaney
@devinmar19	Marie Sommers
@fatfempinup	@just_nadez
Chelsey aka @fatgirl_laughing	@missemn82
Fatima	@anactingangel
Haye Moon	JammieJay
Lia Mcguire @fattyabaddie	@wet_heat
@kellybellyohio	@msgabrielle_3
Helene Thyrsted	@tonicaggiano
@girlcatphotography	@nu_perspective_photography
Tamara Lay	

www.ingramcontent.com/pod-product-compliance
Lightning Source LLC
Chambersburg PA
CBHW051222220526
45473CB00003B/1133